"Drawing from the gospel and her own [experi]ence, Denise Grace Gitsham reminds us [that ...] never come before the divine call to love a[...] *[Politics for People] Who Hate Politics* is a book that every Christian must read."

Arthur C. Brooks
professor, Harvard Kennedy School and Harvard Business School
#1 *New York Times* bestselling author

"Denise's unrelenting passion for Jesus and people is evident to all who come across her path. In this rough-and-tumble business of politics, she has learned to keep her eyes on the prize and serve with excellence and purpose. Her unique experiences, fountain of wisdom, and uncanny kingdom-mindedness have allowed her to have a powerful impact on the lives of many, including my own. I know her words will encourage and inspire you as they have me so many times throughout my career."

Congressman Jodey Arrington

"This book calls on all Americans to rise to a higher standard of behavior, thought, and action as they engage in politics. Denise champions Jesus' core message of love, honor, and truth, making this book a must-read for anyone who shares our heart for unity."

Miles McPherson
pastor of the Rock Church, author, and former defensive back for the San Diego Chargers

"As politics increasingly creeps into every part of our lives, navigating the tricky waters to preserve friendships and family relationships can be difficult—but it is critical to the joy of life. Denise has great advice for steering clear of trouble so that you never lose a friend because of politics."

Dana Perino
Fox News anchor and former White House Press Secretary

"*Politics for People Who Hate Politics* is the most givable book I have read in recent years. I will be giving it for Christmas to ministry partners and even to family. Denise has bridged the gap and created the equivalent of emotional intelligence for politics that I would call 'political intelligence' for the average person like me. I feel so much more equipped to understand and, better yet, have life-giving conversations than I did before reading this book. Many Christians get stuck trying to articulate political subjects. Denise has broken it down so I don't have to, and I will be forever grateful to have not just a book but a spiritual tool in my hand."

Shawn Bolz
TV host, commentator, author, minister, and podcaster
www.bolzministries.com

"Denise Gitsham has done us all an incredible service by writing this book. Hers is a voice of biblical truth that cuts through the rancor and loss of civility that have become a cancer in the United States today. I highly recommend that every American and certainly every believer in the nation read it."

Cindy Jacobs
Generals International

"Denise Gitsham's book, *Politics for People Who Hate Politics*, offers an important cautionary tale for anyone hoping to be both faithful and active in politics. As she illustrates through her own life and career, it is far too easy to be drawn into the bitter partisan battles of our day, and to see a self-righteous, no-holds-barred approach to politics as the only way to win. With so many Christians drawn into the politics of culture war issues from the right and left, it's all too easy to lose sight of our shared calling to love one another with humility rather than to beat one another at all costs. Denise has written a refreshing and self-critical reflection on her own life in politics and why it is so important for people of faith to be willing to put their calling to heal our nation above their partisan loyalties."

Senator Chris Coons

# POLITICS FOR PEOPLE
# WHO HATE POLITICS

# POLITICS FOR PEOPLE WHO HATE POLITICS

**HOW TO ENGAGE WITHOUT LOSING YOUR FRIENDS
OR SELLING YOUR SOUL**

## DENISE GRACE GITSHAM

BETHANYHOUSE
a division of Baker Publishing Group
Minneapolis, Minnesota

Published by Bethany House Publishers
Minneapolis, Minnesota
www.bethanyhouse.com

Bethany House Publishers is a division of
Baker Publishing Group, Grand Rapids, Michigan

Printed in the United States of America

ISBN 978-0-7642-4147-5 (paper)
ISBN 978-0-7642-4229-8 (casebound)
ISBN 978-1-4934-4381-9 (ebook)

Library of Congress Cataloging-in-Publication Control Number: 2023026949

The Author is represented by William K. Jensen Literary Agency.

23  24  25  26  27  28  29      7  6  5  4  3  2  1

This book is dedicated to my parents,
Calvin Henry Ward and Grace Wei Mei Gitsham,
whose love for and loyalty to our nation inspired mine.

# CONTENTS

# FOREWORD

I first met Denise through mutual friends in San Diego while she was running for Congress in California's then-Fifty-second Congressional District. We quickly realized that we shared not only a passion for the welfare of our nation, but more importantly, a deep and abiding faith in Jesus.

Denise, who sadly lost her race, has a sincere desire to see our brothers and sisters in the faith acting like they actually believe in the principles they espouse—principles that sound great in theory, but are difficult to put into action, especially when it comes to politics.

Denise's book is both timely and necessary in this highly divisive era of politics. While the church has historically been a catalyst for positive social and political change, in recent years we've begun to lose our moral and spiritual authority. Instead of bringing the love of Christ into politics, we've let politics affect our love for one another. Is it any wonder, then, that one of the most-cited reasons pastors leave the ministry is "current political divisions"?[1] Nothing and no one is immune from the impact of politics done wrong; not friendships, workplaces, communities, families, or churches—all have been negatively impacted.

Mind you, sharing a faith rarely equates to marching in lock-step on all things political. Christians on the same side of the aisle rarely agree on everything. Even Jesus' disciples quarreled among one another right in front of Him. And whenever they did, Jesus commanded them to do as He wills us to today: be humble, love well, speak truth, and maintain unity in the body of Christ. For our spiritual posture, our hearts, our character, and our love will make a far greater impact on this world than any political position ever will.

This book drives that much-needed reminder home in an era that resists it wholeheartedly. Denise chips away at our resistance by reminding us that we were always meant to live counterculturally. Like our Savior, who was crucified for refusing to give in to political pressure to conform, neither were we meant to fit perfectly into any earthly mold. Whether Republican, Democrat, Independent, or none of the above, our loyalty must remain—first and foremost—to God and God alone.

This book will inspire you to show up as your best self both in and beyond the political sphere. Applying these principles will undoubtedly help us foster the "more perfect union" our Founding Fathers envisioned. But even more importantly, it will improve our relationships with friends, family members, coworkers, and our brothers and sisters in Christ. For when Americans care as deeply about how we show up in politics as what we show up for, we are likelier to shape a nation that we'll be proud to be a part of and preserve it for generations to come.

Senator Tim Scott (R-SC)

# INTRODUCTION

"D . . ." a friend recently texted, "I'm SO OVER politics. I just can't deal with any more opinionated friends and relatives, and I'm so tired of holding my tongue. Been praying for patience, but it's seriously wearing thin. Already dreading the holidays, big time. I know I need to speak up, but I can't seem to do it in a loving way. Also, I'm just not feeling all that loving about people I disagree with right now. So tell me: how do I navigate politics as a Christian without killing someone or going crazy?"

Reading her text, all I could think was "SAME, girl, same." I've asked God the very same questions, similarly avoided certain friends and relatives during election season, and experienced more than my fair share of uncomfortable holiday dinners, all because of politics. And, like my friend, I've ridden the pendulum swing of wanting to speak out and needing to withdraw. Sometimes, it feels like stepping away is the only way to guard my heart, protect my relationships, and save my sanity. But invariably, I find myself jumping back into the fray, unable to stay quiet about the issues that matter most. I thus find myself both loving and hating politics—for what it can do and for what it's become.

It's hard to wholeheartedly embrace politics today, even for someone like me, who's chosen it as her career. Politics have co-opted everything from social media to the 24/7 cable news cycle, and even pop culture. There's no place to hide from everyone's opinions, and no rest for the politically weary, who are . . .

Tired of being vilified for having an opinion.

Tired of walking on eggshells.

Tired of faking agreement to avoid a conflict.

Tired of bomb-throwing social media trolls.

Tired of unfriending and being unfriended.

Tired of arguing.

Tired of being silenced and dismissed.

Tired of "lowest common denominator" discourse.

And tired of feeling . . . tired.

I remember a time in the not-too-distant past when partisan bantering was fun. I've always had a good mix of Democratic and Republican friends, and a debate, for me, was always a learning experience. I love having my views challenged and my perspectives broadened. Previously, those conversations never felt threatening.

But something's changed as of late. Politics have become personal—dangerous, even. People are now tarred and feathered for holding opinions the ever-changing masses deem "politically incorrect" or "woke." Others are physically harmed—even killed—for standing on the "wrong" side of a protest line. Some are fired for holding fast to their political convictions. Still others are labeled "fascists," "commies," and "RINOs" for taking stands that are too far right, left, or centrist in their accusers' minds.

While the recent uptick in political dissension alarms us today, none of this is entirely surprising or new. At various points in our nation's history, people have taken up literal arms to fight for their political beliefs, risking death, destruction, and liveli-hoods in the process. But what's new and heartbreaking for me—a twenty-plus-year veteran of politics and a follower of Christ for more than thirty—is witnessing *Christians* engage in politics the way the world does: as a blood sport, rather than as bondservants of Christ.

The Bible is very clear about how Christians are to show up in this world, regardless of the circumstances we find ourselves in. Jesus says that a watching world will know Him because of our love—for those with whom we agree, as well as for those with whom we do not (John 13:35). Humility, kindness, and love are the hallmarks of our faith. So when aspects of our political engagement fall short of those standards, we willfully sacrifice our witness at the world's expense—and ours.

Before I go any further, it's vitally important that I clarify my heart posture in writing this book: everything I've writ-ten stems from a position of humility and repentance, rather than of admonition or judgment. I still struggle with loving my political opponents as much as anyone else who's passionate about our nation, its policies, and its leadership. I'm often just as quick to justify my words and actions—however unloving they may be—by labeling them "truth." I've been known to troll politicians I don't like with nasty comments and commentary. And I've engaged in more than a few smear campaigns against political opponents, all in the name of winning. I am, after all, a product of Washington, DC.

But because I am a believer, God's influence on my life must be greater than culture's. I am called to obey His command-ments no matter where I live, what I do, or "how things are done." Moreover, He's *empowered* me to obey Him, so I'm actually capable of doing all that He asks. That leaves me with no excuses for living any other way.

The fact is, God cares as much about my obedience to Him as He does about the policies I fight for. My job is to speak the truth in love, to honor God, and to love others through my words and actions, no matter how I am treated in return. There is no political outcome important enough to justify acting any differently—for me or for any other believer.

If the church aligns its actions with these truths, this divisive moment in history could offer a once-in-a-generation opportunity for us to become a unifying force for our nation. While others destroy one another, believers can flip the script on politics as usual by loving those we disagree with. The light of Jesus' love always shines brightest in the darkness, and in this moment, we can shine brighter than ever before by being *for* people, even when we are *against* what they stand for.

This book is an invitation to participate in our broken political system, and to change it from the inside out by engaging in politics in a manner worthy of Christ. It won't be easy—nothing worth doing ever is—but with God's help, we can become the glue that holds our fragile republic together and makes politics more palatable for everyone involved.

# INDIVISIBLE

A house divided against itself cannot stand.
—Abraham Lincoln (based on Mark 3:25)

Our first president, George Washington, refused to run as a member of any political party. He wanted to be a president to *all* Americans. Washington firmly believed that political parties would divide and destroy our fledgling nation, and he knew that unity was essential to its survival.

Washington's fundamental concern was that Americans would vote based on party loyalties rather than the overarching interests of our nation. Once that happened, he predicted, a "spirit of revenge" would accompany it, and enable the rise of "cunning, ambitious, and unprincipled men." He said the "spirit of party . . . agitates the community with ill-founded jealousies and false alarms, kindles the animosity of one part against another, [and] foments occasionally riot and insurrection."[1]

Sound familiar?

Washington spoke from personal experience: his family had fled England precisely to *avoid* civil war there. He and other Founding Fathers believed that political parties were monarchical vestiges that had no place in our budding republic. James Madison, for example, wrote that a "wellconstructed Union" should "break and control the violence of faction."[2] Alexander Hamilton called political parties the "most fatal disease" of popular governments.[3] And John Adams's greatest fear was "Division of the Republick into two great Parties, each arranged under its Leader, and concerting Measures in opposition to each other."[4]

Despite their warnings, two dominant political parties quickly rose to power. In 1791, Alexander Hamilton, Mr. "Factions are Fatal" himself, founded the Federalist Party. A year later, Thomas Jefferson founded the Anti-Federalist Party to oppose everything Hamilton and his followers stood for. And in the institutionalization of these two parties, Americans' hatred of politics took root.

Today, this hatred thrives. Biologists, psychologists, and sociologists offer myriad reasons for its existence, ranging from our desire to reduce computational complexity to our intrinsic desire for hierarchical status. These rationales make our hatred of politics *seem* inevitable, but it isn't. As Christians, we *can* and *must* transcend our basest human instincts to forge a unifying path forward.

## The Making of a Politico

As a reminder, when I say "we," I'm pointing the finger at myself. I've been a Christian for most of my life, as well as a conservative. Politics run deep in our family, and being a Republican has always felt like a birthright. One of my earliest childhood memories is of sitting on my father's knee, celebrating Ronald

Reagan's first presidential victory. I've spent every election night since rooting for my favorite Republican candidates.

My own political career began in my freshman year of high school when I threw myself into student government. I was elected class president four years in a row and learned the nuts and bolts of grassroots politicking in the process. As a high schooler, I didn't run on a party platform, but I did learn how to distinguish myself from other candidates in ways that were equal parts effective and ridiculous. Case in point: I ordered thousands of customized fortune cookies that read, "Vote for Denise: she's one smart cookie," which I'm pretty sure got me over the finish line every single year.

In college, I leveraged the skills I'd gleaned in high school to get elected as president of my freshman class. The lure of holding office, however, quickly wore off. Student body elections, I realized, were mere popularity contests, better suited for high schoolers. I was far more interested in debating classmates and professors on the virtues of conservatism. I had well-formed opinions that I was happy to defend against anyone who disagreed with me. And boy, did I have opportunities to do so: as one of the few conservatives at my college, I was regularly challenged to consider perspectives I'd never even encountered before. Over time, I learned to value and respect those who held differing opinions, so long as theirs were rooted in rationality and truth. Their views didn't change my firmly held beliefs, but I could appreciate how and why they arrived at theirs.

After graduating from college, I dove headfirst into a career in politics. My college mentor encouraged me to join a real campaign after I ran (and won) a mock congressional campaign in my senior year. At the time, America was gearing up for the 2000 presidential election, and nothing seemed worthier of my energy and attention than helping to elect the next leader of the free world. So in August of 1999, I left the coast of Maine to join what was described to me as a "start-up presidential campaign" in Austin, Texas. With tons of enthusiasm, zero experience, and a 24/7 work ethic, I began interning for then-Governor George W. Bush's chief campaign strategist, Karl Rove.

I loved the campaign trail and felt as though I'd found my calling. I spent every day advocating for issues that squared with my conservative ideology, and I fought hard for the hearts and minds of every constituent. The harder I worked, however, the more convinced I was that everything we stood for was right, while everything our opponents stood for was wrong. Gone was my ability to consider issues from any perspective other than those I fought for. At one point, another professor that I'd admired in college reached out to me, challenging our candidate's position on an issue. Being on the front lines of the campaign, I had no desire or ability to see things from his perspective, much less respond to his email. Every criticism he levied against our campaign felt like a personal attack, which was my first indication that my own identity was enmeshed with my party's. I didn't realize it at the time, but I was becoming a party hack.

This merging of identities caused me to double down on my ideological territorialism, which changed the lens through which I viewed the world. Rather than see things through the objective lens of biblical truth, I categorized every political perspective as right or wrong, based on how they squared with my party's beliefs. Doing so freed my mind from debating issues and enabled it to focus on winning. It also helped me rationalize the questionable campaign tactics I sometimes employed with an "ends justify means" mentality.

As my identity changed, so did my social circle. Reducing computational complexity was a skill my overtaxed brain clung to for survival. Since complexity stemmed from engaging my liberal friends in conversation, I stopped talking with those whose perspectives differed from mine. My college professor was just one of many people I cut out of my life while working on the campaign trail. I simply didn't have the bandwidth, energy, or desire to consider other perspectives or defend my own. "We'll pick up where we left off *after* we win," I told myself, knowing full well we wouldn't.

After two grueling Florida recounts and a hotly contested Supreme Court case, we finally won the election. In December of 2000, I moved to Washington to work on the Presidential Inaugural Committee. Shortly thereafter, I accepted a position at the White House, where I quickly learned the difference between campaigning and governing.

As White House staffers, our official mandates changed. No longer did we serve a party or a candidate; rather, we swore oaths to uphold the Constitution in service to our country. Every American was our constituent, regardless of who they voted for. To me, this was a welcome change after a long and divisive election. As much as I loved campaigning, the recount process led to extreme politicking that tore our nation apart. I saw my job as knitting America back together.

No matter how hard we tried working with those across the aisle, however, partisan rancor prevailed. As President Bush came under increasing attack, we defaulted to our old battle positions and went back into campaign mode. It seemed like our only option at the time, which seeded a hatred in my heart for that which I once loved.

I learned hard lessons in my first few years in Washington that intensified my growing disdain for politics. The first was that no matter how rosy things were between individual politicians, Republicans always sided with Republicans, and Democrats with Democrats. Breaking with your own party to vote with the other yielded a clear and definitive outcome: a one-way ticket back to the state you came from. There were no incentives to vote your conscience if your conscience deviated from your party's. As such, many people with innovative and unifying ideas were prevented from ever acting on or sharing them.

The second lesson I learned was that truth takes on a malleable nature, and only becomes "truth" when it's presented by the "right" politician. As someone who values truth and finds it in the Word of God, it became harder and harder for me to adhere to party platforms—not because they were anti-Christian, per se, but because their roots were in secular, rather than sacred, truths. I have no problem with worldly wisdom; I just don't want to spend my life fighting over issues that have no eternal value or worth.

The third lesson I learned was that humility, a hallmark of Christ and those who follow Him, is a sign of weakness in politics. To admit one's own wrongdoing or to acknowledge that one might not have answers to every problem is never allowed. Showing humility is not only considered weak in Washington; it's a death knell for any aspiring politico's career. That leaves believers like me in a bind; we can either choose to be like Jesus and stay in the background or garner influence for ourselves by being a know-it-all. The tension I felt juggling these two extremes made me feel like a liar and a charlatan.

Seeing no practical alternative to politics as usual, I did what I saw modeled around me and became part of the problem, rather than the solution. As I did, I noticed that partisanship grew more, rather than less, extreme. Those of us who had the power to change this reality chose not to. Rather than elevating the political dialogue, we fought fire with fire. And in so doing, we perpetuated the same division that plagues us today, and makes us hate politics all the more.

## Politics Today

I wish I could say that things have gotten better over time, but things have only grown worse. Over the past two decades, partisan messaging has so permeated our culture that election season is now a year-round, 24/7 reality. Political agendas are embedded in every cultural conversation, with nowhere to escape. Americans have responded by barricading themselves behind partisan walls and engaging in trench warfare—not against foreign enemies, but against each other.

It's hardly a surprise, then, that recent presidential elections have been the most bitterly divided in modern history. In 2020, both Biden and Trump supporters believed that differences between them were about more than just politics and policies. A month before the election, 80% of registered voters in both camps said that their differences with the other side were about "core American values," and approximately 90% worried that a victory by the other party would lead to "lasting harm" in the United States.[5]

Social scientists have also found that our heightened political division is due to our alignment of identity with politics. Politics have morphed from *what* we believe to *who* we think we are.[6] Race, religion, and ideology have become so closely aligned with partisan identity that it's hard to separate them from each other. Accordingly, we've migrated from believing that "we're right" and "they're wrong," to believing that "we're good" and "they're bad." And when our divisions become rooted in *who* we think we are rather than *what* we believe, common ground becomes nearly impossible to forge.

The only *good* news is that Americans on both sides of the aisle claim to *want* a more unified nation—not conformity, but unity with their fellow countrymen. A poll from the 2020 election season revealed that 86% of Trump supporters and 89% of Biden supporters said that their preferred candidate, if elected, should address the needs of *all* Americans, "even if it means disappointing some of his supporters."[7] In 2018, 90% felt that the division in our nation was a "serious" or "very serious" problem that needed to be addressed.[8] And another, more recent poll found that 75% of Americans believe that in order to "restore peace and unity we need leaders to model kindness and understanding, even with people they strongly disagree with."[9] Which begs the question: *If an overwhelming majority of Americans want to see our nation unified, and Christians are commanded and empowered to unify, why aren't we leading the way?*

## Called to Unify

Unity within the body of Christ is nonnegotiable to God. Scripture instructs us, in 179 verses woven throughout the Old Testament and New, to live in peace, love, and unity with God and each other. A sampling of these verses highlights God's heart for unity and emphasizes its essentiality to our primary mission in this world, which is spreading the gospel.

> I appeal to you, brothers and sisters . . . that there be no divisions among you, but that you might be perfectly united in mind and thought.
>
> 1 Corinthians 1:10

> May the God who gives endurance and encouragement give you the same attitude of mind toward each other that Christ Jesus had, so that with one mind and one voice you may glorify the God and Father of our Lord Jesus Christ.
>
> Romans 15:5–6

> Do we not all have one Father? Did not one God create us? Why do we profane the covenant of our ancestors by being unfaithful to one another?
>
> Malachi 2:10

> Strive for full restoration, encourage one another, be of one mind, live in peace.
>
> 2 Corinthians 13:11

Also in Judah the hand of God was on the people to give them unity of mind to carry out what the king and his officials had ordered.

2 Chronicles 30:12

Make my joy complete by being like-minded having the same love, being one in spirit and of one mind.

Philippians 2:2

Be completely humble and gentle; be patient, bearing with one another in love. Make every effort to keep the unity of the Spirit through the bond of peace. There is one body and one Spirit, just as you were called to one hope when you were called; one Lord, one faith, one baptism; one God and Father of all, who is over all and through all and in all.

Ephesians 4:2–6

I pray also for those who will believe in me through their message, that all of them may be one, Father, just as you are in me and I am in you. May they also be in us, so that the world may believe that you have sent me.

John 17:20–23

These verses remind us that unity is more than just a goal to be pursued for its own sake. Rather, unity is the identifying characteristic of a life lived in submission to God. As the gospel of John highlights, our unity, which stems from our love, honor, and service toward one another, is what distinguishes us as Christians. When we don't love and honor others well, strife, hatred, and division consume us, ruining our credibility and witness to the world.

## Victimization as Justification

One of the primary ways we justify our divisiveness is by blaming others for starting it. Saying that we *want* to be unified, while doing nothing to initiate such unity ourselves, shifts the onus of responsibility from our shoulders onto theirs. "They're just so close-minded/hateful/blind," we tell ourselves, as if the actions and attitudes of others excuse our own lack of initiative and obedience to God. My question to those who buy into this mindset is first, why should we expect others to do what God has directed *us* to do? And second, is our obedience *that* dependent on how the world around us operates? If so, we're in deep trouble—not only regarding how we politick, but in every aspect of our lives.

Blaming others for our own disobedience renders us "victims," which helps us justify doing anything we deem necessary in order to protect our families, our livelihoods, and ourselves. When we feel powerless, we feel justified doing whatever we "must"—which is why victims can't lead; they can only react and follow. That's also why they're so inclined to gravitate toward others who feel the same way; they find strength in each other rather than in Christ's promises. As mob mentalities and group thinking permeate the body of Christ, our "mind of Christ" disappears. "Victims" become "oppressors" by mirroring the behaviors of their political enemies. And Christians end up joining others in sinking to lowest-common-denominator behaviors, all in the name of "survival."

Those with victim mentalities often gravitate toward leaders who project strength, authority, and power—all the characteristics they're lacking in themselves. They look to human authorities who promise to provide for and protect them, rather than trusting God to fulfill His promises. Victimized electorates choose rulers who magnify our fears and turn us against those who oppose them. "Follow me!" they say, and we do . . . right over a cliff.

To top it all off, "victims" are some of the most miserable people to be around. They embody everything the Bible tells us not to be—selfish, prideful, and divisive. They act disrespectfully and take no responsibility for their own actions, justifying the harm they cause by yelling, "They started it!"

The thought of grown-ups uttering something you'd only expect out of a kindergartener's mouth would be comical if it weren't actually true. But sadly, it is; just look at the talking heads on TV, who blame, criticize, and slander those with whom they disagree. Rarely do they appeal to our best selves, never do they tell the whole truth, and precious few strike a peaceful or honoring tone. Deflecting responsibility, inciting fear, and fomenting division are their tickets to power, and we consume what they throw our way—hook, line, and sinker.

Again, I speak from personal experience because I, too, was guilty of buying into their hype. I adopted a victim mentality, and rather than responding honorably, I responded in kind, while laying blame at the feet of others. I was a Christian then, just as I am now, and I should have known better. But it took years of experience and hours of prayerful reflection to learn what I know today: we are always victors, and never victims, when we belong to Christ.

## Unity in Action

According to the book of Proverbs, the Lord detests "a person who stirs up conflict in the community" (6:19). In Romans, Paul warns the early church to "watch out for people who cause divisions. . . . Stay away from them. Such people are not serving Christ our Lord; they are serving their own personal interests" (16:17–18 NLT). And in his first letter to the Corinthians, Paul calls the church out for being "still of the flesh. For while there is jealousy and strife among you, are you not of the flesh and behaving only in a human way?" (3:3 ESV). These verses and others like it emphasize God's hatred of division. Nevertheless, many Christians ignore them and allow themselves to be manipulated by politicians into becoming instruments of division themselves.

Thankfully, not every politician operates this way. One standout is Senator Tim Scott of South Carolina. A Black Republican who grew up in the Deep South, his life has been threatened so many times by people on both sides of the aisle that he's had to hire bodyguards to protect him. If anyone has a reason to play the victim card, it's definitely him.

Nevertheless, he rejects the label outright. He knows he isn't a victim, but rather a victor in Christ (Romans 8:37). Rather than letting others define him, he defines himself according to the Word of God. No matter what others say about him, he responds honorably. His ability to do so is rooted in his identity in Christ, which renders his approach to lawmaking very different from what we normally see in Washington. Unlike those who view their mission as promoting a partisan agenda, Senator Scott views his mission as expressing God's love to Americans through the policies he promotes. By emphasizing godly principles over partisan politics, he's able to reach across party lines to solve problems in a bipartisan manner. Rather than dividing Congress further, he unites his fellow senators based on the common goals they share.

Senator Scott is one of the few leaders I know who avoids blaming the other side for everything that's wrong with America. He doesn't have to point fingers to make himself look better. By standing for unity rather than division and leading with humility and grace, he's become one of the most well-liked and effective members of Congress.

Like Senator Scott, I know that succumbing to a victim mentality leads me down a dangerous political path. And yet, for years, I played the political blame game rather than taking initiative to bridge the partisan gap. *How could a Christian like me have been so wrong-headed in her approach to politics?* you might wonder. I attribute it to the same spirit that brought partisanship into existence two hundred years ago, and continues to fracture our country, communities, and churches today.

## Holy v. Political Spirits

The Bible says that when we become Christians, we receive a helper who takes up residence in our hearts (John 14:16). That helper is the Holy Spirit, who empowers us to live like Jesus. Scripture says that evidence of the Holy Spirit's influence on our lives is expressed in love, joy, peace, forbearance, kindness, goodness, faithfulness, gentleness, and self-control (Galatians 5:22–23). Since every Christian has the Holy Spirit living inside of them, we are all empowered to live this way, all of the time.

The political spirit, on the other hand, emanates from culture and exalts politics over God as the answer to our problems. It causes us to be self-seeking, prideful, and manipulative in pursuing our own interests. And it seeks to corrupt our souls by tempting us to pledge our loyalties to false idols, while demanding "uniformity through the pressures of fear, shame, and control."[10]

The political spirit emerges in every age and culture. It was on full display when the tower of Babel was built, when the Israelites sought a human king, and when the Pharisees partnered with the Romans to murder Jesus. It's what led Judas to betray Christ. It's what caused Absalom to usurp his father's throne. It made Saul murderously jealous of David. And it's led to the division and destruction of every kingdom, church, and nation in human history.

Just as the fruits of the Holy Spirit are evident in fully submitted lives, so are those of the political spirit. Kris Vallotton of Bethel Church tells us that the political spirit:

☑ Persuades people to spiritualize the demeaning of people of different persuasions,

☑ Convinces people that they are justified in applying a different standard of behavior toward those whom they deem wrong,

☑ Convinces people to assign the blame for all the problems of society to one people group,

☑ Causes people to redefine dishonoring attitudes as virtuous attributes, and

☑ Causes people to create an us-and-them mentality.[11]

As I read through this list, I was struck by how many of these attributes I identify with. This makes me not only the worst of sinners, but also the most qualified to speak on the matter. Since the Holy and political spirits are at odds with each other, they cannot coexist in our lives, which means we're either serving one or the other. As followers of Christ, we must choose which spirit we submit to, for "no one can serve two masters" (Matthew 6:24). The question thus becomes, which spirit will we choose?

## Commandments, Pleas, and Warnings

In the Old Testament, Isaiah prophesied that Jesus would be called the "Prince of Peace" (9:6). Seven hundred years later, Jesus proved who He was by living up to His moniker. Over the course of His life, Jesus sacrificed everything, including himself, to bring peace to mankind. He didn't do so by avoiding conflict, appeasing wrongdoers, or giving in to evil. Rather He stood on God's truth and proactively engaged in peacemaking with a warrior's mentality and a servant's heart.

As Christians, we are empowered to follow in Jesus' footsteps by the Holy Spirit living inside of us. We are not only instructed by God to "seek peace and pursue it" (Psalm 34:14), but we also have the power and authority to bring it into fruition. The question is whether we're *willing* to submit our earthly desires to God by pursuing His peace rather than political division. And that's a question worth pondering since peacemaking isn't for the faint of heart.

It's far easier to pick a side and stick with it than it is to seek common ground. Peacemaking is rarely a popular stance, even among Christians who agree on its importance. As Benjamin Franklin noted, "BLESSED *are the Peacemakers*, is I suppose to be understood in the other World; for in this [world] they are more frequently *cursed*."[12] Based on our current state of affairs, it appears nothing has changed since he wrote these words in 1781.

That's because everything about peacemaking flies in the face of culture. Nothing scares Satan more than a united body of believers, so the Enemy always attacks our unity first. Christians can only fight back by proactively pursuing peace, which is why the apostle Paul urges us to keep our distance from those who foster division (Romans 16:17): to protect the church—and our nation—from destroying ourselves from within.

Lest we dismiss Paul's words as mere suggestions, I suggest studying what happens to those who embrace division. Consider the Old Testament character named Korah, who initiated a rebellion against Moses and Aaron by assembling 250 men to oppose their leadership. When they confronted the brothers, Moses and Aaron replied, "When you complain against [us], it is really against the Lord that you and your followers are rebelling" (Numbers 16:11 GNT). Moses told Korah that the next morning God would show him who He'd chosen as their leader. When morning came, God sent an earthquake that killed Korah and his family, a bolt of lightning to destroy the leaders who'd sided with them, and a plague that wiped out the other 14,700 people who'd grumbled against them. God took it upon himself to eliminate those who'd chosen division over unity (Numbers 16).

There are many lessons we can glean from this story, but the primary one is this: whenever we choose division, we step outside of God's will. We may think we have good reasons for doing so, but God cares more about our unity than our frustrations. Seeking God's help in loving those we'd rather separate from is a safer, more honoring response. And if you doubt the truth of this statement, just ask Korah and those who followed him.

## Becoming a Unifying Force

I wish I could say that peace and unity were the primary motivators for my political engagement, but until recently they simply weren't. For years, I bought into the lie that doing whatever it took—going negative, exaggerating, smearing my opponents, and misrepresenting their platforms—was the only way to win. There were times when my conscience was tweaked, but the ends always seemed to justify the means—especially when winning was synonymous with achieving the "right" policy outcome. What could be more justifiable than doing whatever it took to bring God's will into fruition? Surely, I rationalized, He would overlook *how* I did things, so long as my *intentions* were good.

Thankfully, God has corrected my flawed thinking on this matter. Over the years, He's taught me that my obedience is what pleases Him most. This realization led me to ask God to expose every part of my life that wasn't fully submitted to Him. In response, He highlighted the parts of my heart that preferred division over unity and helped change them to be more like His. By laying down my old ways of doing things, I've gained a new appreciation for the power of unity, as well as an inner peace that indicates that I'm finally doing things God's way. This feeling has renewed my love of politics by making me feel like I'm doing something helpful rather than tearing our nation apart.

As transformative as these revelations are for me, imagine how impactful they'd be if they spread throughout the church! As the single largest voting bloc in America, Christians would transform politics if we could just bring ourselves to unify around the principles of God. A unified church would not only strengthen us politically, but spiritually as well. The result would be a net positive impact on all Americans—turning politics from something we run from to something we can finally embrace.

## REFLECTION

1. Are you more of a unifying or divisive force in politics?
2. How do you feel about those who have a different political opinion than you do?
3. What can you do in your personal capacity to help bridge the partisan divide?

## PRAYER

*Lord, use me to unite believers and by extension our beloved nation. Help me to see my brothers and sisters on the other side of the aisle as family rather than foes. Replace my partisan beliefs with kingdom principles and unite our hearts around your truth. Help us change this nation for the better by making us truly indivisible. In Jesus' name, Amen.*

## 2

# IDENTITY POLITICS

Define yourself radically as one beloved by God. This is the
true self. Every other identity is illusion.

—Brennan Manning, *Abba's Child*

In 2015, I stepped into the arena as a first-time candidate. Running for political office was a lifelong dream, something that had been on my vision board and prayer list for decades. More specifically, I felt called to run for *Congress*. Given that all my governmental experience was in Washington, DC, federal issues were those I knew best and felt most passionate about.

In choosing to run for such a "big" office, I ignored the advice of those who encouraged me to take baby steps by running for city council first. Their advice was practical and well-meaning; I had zero percent name identification, was relatively new to San Diego, and was only thirty-eight years old. Furthermore, I'd chosen to run against an incumbent who'd been in office for twenty years and was married to one of the wealthiest women in San Diego. The odds were stacked against me, but since I knew what it would take to run and win, I didn't let the enormity of the challenge hold me back.

I spent my first few months on the campaign trail raising money, meeting community leaders, and learning about the issues that mattered most to my constituents. While I spent the majority of my time campaigning in my district, I occasionally flew across the country, attending events hosted by former colleagues and friends with whom I'd worked in Washington, DC. Because they were seasoned politicos, their confidence in my candidacy buoyed my spirits, and, given how skeptical my San Diego friends were, I desperately needed their encouragement.

## "Latina Superstar"

One such event was a dinner that my friend Rebecca Contreras hosted in Austin, Texas. I first met Rebecca in Austin when I was the Hispanic Coalitions Coordinator on Governor Bush's presidential campaign. I assumed the role accidentally; prior to that, I'd been interning (for free) for eight months. In month nine, I finally mustered the courage to ask my boss, campaign strategist Karl Rove, for a paid position. I knew that I was thoroughly expendable, given the thousands of résumés that poured into our office each week, and that even asking him for a paid position put me at risk of losing my unpaid internship. But I had no choice other than to ask, having burned the candle at both ends for months, selling gym memberships after hours to support my political habit.

After what felt like an eternity but was actually a week or two, Karl approached me with a twinkle in his eye. My heart raced with excitement as I realized my dream of becoming a *salaried* staffer was about to come true.

"We've got the perfect job for you, Denise. It's gonna be fabulous!" Karl said with all his signature enthusiasm. "You're gonna be our new Hispanic Coalitions Coordinator!" Karl paused and waited for my reaction. Given how long and hard I'd worked as his intern, I wasn't about to state the not-so-obvious—that I wasn't Hispanic, but rather half-Chinese. I couldn't say no, and didn't want to either since who knew when another opportunity might arise? So I flashed a big smile, nodded excitedly, and said, "¡Sí, señor! ¡Gracias!"

It was in this role that I first met Rebecca, who was one of Governor Bush's senior aides and a proud Latina. There's so much I admire about Rebecca, but above all, I love the way she uses her God-given talent and connections to help others achieve their full purpose and potential. She's always had a knack for putting the right people in the right place at the right time, which is why she served the President so well in the White House Office of Presidential Personnel.

After she left Washington, I kept in touch with Rebecca and told her I'd let her know when I visited her hometown of Austin. In October 2015, I scheduled a trip to the Austin City Limits music festival a few weeks before I planned to announce my candidacy for Congress. Rebecca knew about it and wanted to help, so she invited my friends and me over to her house for dinner.

We showed up casually dressed and ready to enjoy a low-key evening with Rebecca and her husband, David. In the short walk from her front door to her living room, however, we were surprised to see a number of other people at her house. Rebecca was a great hostess, but it seemed odd that she'd invite others when I thought she was just planning on having the three of us over. Stranger still was the fact that everyone seemed particularly interested in talking to me.

It wasn't until we settled into dinner that I got a sense of what was really going on. Rebecca clinked her glass with a fork and asked everyone to quiet down so that she could say a few words. "As you know, I'm all about supporting our community," she opened. As I looked around, I realized she was referencing the Hispanic community, which was well represented in the room. Rebecca continued, "Tonight, I've invited you over for more than just a great meal. I want you all to meet my amiga and rising Latina superstar: Denise Gitsham!"

My friends looked at me and blinked hard. For a moment, I froze. What could I say after such a generous introduction and gesture? After what felt like an eternity, I gathered myself and regained my composure. I wasn't about to embarrass my friend in her own house. But in that moment, I realized Rebecca was the only person I'd worked with at the White House who hadn't gotten the memo on my true identity.

To be fair, it wasn't the first time I'd been mistaken for Latina. Growing up in rural California, nobody quite knew what to make of my ethnicity, and most assumed I was Hispanic. My childhood best friend was Mexican, many of our close family friends were Latino, and most of the kids I grew up with were of Hispanic origin. Ironically, even Chinese nationals mistook me for Latina. I lost count of the number of times I was spoken to in Spanish when I worked in Beijing's diplomatic community. However, this was the first time a close friend had mistaken my ethnic identity.

In her defense, Rebecca had every reason to believe I was who she thought I was. When she met me on the campaign trail, I looked and played the role of Governor Bush's Hispanic Coalitions Coordinator to a T. As I saw it, it was *my* job to conform to Latino voters, not the other way around. I learned as much as I could about Hispanic history, values, and culture, surrounded myself with Latino advisors, and became close friends with my Hispanic colleagues on the campaign trail. And I fought hard to ensure that the Latino community's interests were well represented both during and after the campaign. In many respects, I felt like a bona fide Latina inside.

Which underscores the point of this chapter: when we look, talk, think, and act a certain way, it's easy to forget—and for others to mistake—who we *really* are. When others have expectations of us, or we're asked to take on a role, we can get so swept up in who we're trying to be that we can easily forget our God-given identities.

All of this seems harmless enough—laughable even—in the context of a campaign. I mean, who's ever heard of a half-Chinese girl being mistaken for a "rising Latina superstar"?! But this example teaches a not-so-funny point: when we let others—whether culture, our jobs, our affiliations, or our friends—override our spiritual identities, we can unintentionally act in ways that misrepresent the person God created us to be.

In some situations, conforming to others' expectations is an appropriate and honoring thing to do. For example, I'd never show up at a wedding in a swimsuit, laugh at a funeral, or attempt to high-five the president. That's because I never want to embarrass myself (or get tackled by the Secret Service), and I always want to honor others. But in other situations, where I'm trying to fit in with, please, or win people over, conformity becomes borderline dangerous. Acting, talking, or engaging in a manner that is contrary to my true nature changes my identity from the outside in. And when it does, it undermines my ability to be everything God has called me to be.

## The Dangers of People-Pleasing

When I first arrived in Austin to work on the Bush campaign, my only goal was to serve God by supporting the candidate I thought would best represent Him. Governor George W. Bush fit the bill perfectly: not only was he a man of deep faith, but he also had a reputation for being a uniter, not a divider. These were two of the many reasons I loved working for him. But unlike other campaign staffers who were lifelong party activists, I was a total newbie. For me, politics were a means, rather than an end, for achieving my goal. When I arrived at campaign headquarters, I was willing to do anything—make coffee, go for lunch runs, fax and file for months on end—all for the privilege of being a part of the team.

Soon after I started, however, I noticed others being promoted faster than me and realized that they were more vocally partisan than I was. I was just as conservative, but far less "political." When I realized that being me simply wasn't cutting it, I decided to change. Eventually, I morphed into a mini-Ann Coulter: a take-no-prisoners politico with the fiery rhetoric, zero-sum-game mentality, and seek-and-destroy intentions to match my new persona. My focus shifted from unifying America to beating the Democrats—precisely what you'd expect from a political activist in training.

I had gone into politics with the purest of intentions—my purpose clear and identity intact. But working in an environment where I didn't fit in made me question my value and self-worth. Like a city girl trading her Prada slingbacks for a pair of Lucchese boots, I gave in to the palpable and pathetic desire to fit in. Within months, I was acting, talking, and thinking like a campaign lackey while engaging in behaviors that belied my true identity.

Sadly, I've seen this phenomenon play out a million times over the course of my political career. In an industry centered on people-pleasing, folks are far more inclined to go with the flow than to resist it. Sadly, this is true for believers as well—even when "the flow" undermines everything we believe in.

Scripture has harsh words for people like me, whose selfish ambition led to people-pleasing and made me sacrifice my witness to get ahead. As the Bible says, pleasing people is anathema to God, and the fear of man is a snare (Proverbs 29:25). That's why the apostle Paul urges us to please God and not people (1 Thessalonians 2:4) and says that if we seek to please man, then we *cannot* please God (Galatians 1:10).

Jesus himself addressed the futility of people-pleasing before a crowd of uber-religious Pharisees, saying, "I'm not interested in crowd approval. . . . Because I know you and your crowds. I know that love, especially God's love, is not on your working agenda. I came with the authority of my Father, and you either dismiss me or avoid me. If another came, acting self-important, you would welcome him with open arms. How do you expect to get anywhere with God when you spend all your time jockeying for position with each other, ranking your rivals and ignoring God?" (John 5:41–44 MSG). In these verses, Jesus makes the point that looking horizontally—that is, to others for approval—keeps us from looking vertically—that is, to God for His.

## Identity Crisis

Whenever we find ourselves horizontally rather than vertically oriented, we're bound to suffer an identity crisis. Nevertheless, this phrase is used so often that it makes identity crises seem innocuous and customary. I mean, aren't we all just trying to figure out where we fit into this world?

Perhaps, but some of the gravest tragedies in human history have stemmed from identity crises. For example, the 1994 Rwandan Civil War stemmed from caste and class identities assigned by German colonists that led to the genocide of over half a million Tutsi minorities at the hands of Hutu militia members. While Rwanda was a colony, the identities of both groups were reshaped and mythologized, providing the basis for anti-Tutsi propaganda that Hutus used to justify their brutality. It didn't matter to either group that they shared the same cultural, linguistic, and tribal roots; in their minds, they were enemies because the colonists said they were.

Identity crises also led to the Cultural Revolution in China, which lasted a decade and resulted in the murder of millions of innocent people. During Mao's reign, the Chinese government brainwashed its citizens into believing that educated people were evil and greedy, while peasants were virtuous and good. Consequently, the lower class turned on the upper class, resulting in massacres, cannibalism, executions, and imprisonments. At the root of this violence was an identity assigned to the Chinese people by a power-hungry leader whose death finally brought the revolution to an end.

Lest we think ourselves immune, it's worth pointing out that some of our godliest heroes have also fallen prey to identity-based lies. King David, whom God called His friend, experienced unparalleled intimacy with the Father. Nevertheless, he suffered an identity crisis when he believed himself to be above God's law and justified taking another man's wife. In a matter of months, King David went from being a just, wise, and moral leader to being someone God never intended him to be: an adulterer and murderer. While those closest to him, with the exception of Nathan, likely fed this delusion, it was David who ultimately chose to deceive himself.

Moses, too, had serious identity issues. While Moses lived a privileged life in Pharaoh's palace, he never quite embraced God's leadership calling on his life. So when God called on Moses to lead His people out of Egypt, He also assured him that he was equipped with everything he needed to lead. Nevertheless, Moses clung to his poor self-image and filled his own mind with doubt: "Who am I," he asked, "that I should bring forth the children of Israel out of Egypt?" (Exodus 3:11 KJV). Moses' identity crisis plagued him throughout his life and ultimately caused him to act in a manner that prevented him from entering the Promised Land.

Nor were identity crises confined to those living in Old Testament times. Even those who knew Jesus personally questioned who they really were. Take, for example, Peter, "the rock" upon whom Jesus said His church would be built. When the going got tough, Peter freaked out and acted like an unbeliever. In a matter of hours, he went from professing his undying loyalty to Jesus, to denying that he even knew Him. If *that* doesn't qualify as an identity crisis, I don't know what does.

## Identity Politics and Tribalism

In the political world, identity crises represent two sides of the same coin: identity politics and tribalism.

*Identity politics* is a term that was coined in 1977 to give Black women who felt ignored by the white feminist movement an opportunity to rally others to join them in political activism. Today, the term is used to describe a political approach taken by the left that "signif[ies] a wide range of political activity and theorizing founded in the shared experiences of injustice of members of certain social groups."[1]

Tribalism, on the other hand, is defined as "a very strong feeling of loyalty to a political or social group" that causes its members to "support them [in] whatever they do."[2] This term has generally been used to describe those on the right, most recently as a way of describing President Trump's supporters. Tribalism, however, long predates the rise of our forty-fifth president.

In the 1980s, Americans put their tribalism on full display when they were overwhelmingly supportive of a "Reagan proposal" for nuclear disarmament until researchers posed the same exact proposal and attributed it to Mikhail Gorbachev.[3] A 2003 study showed that liberal college students were beholden to tribalism when they changed their opinions about a generous welfare policy they initially championed after they were told that it was favored by Republicans.[4] And in 2012, Republican Senator Voinovich described an atmosphere of tribalism within the Republican Senatorial Caucus by stating that if President Obama was for something, then "we had to be against it."[5]

While tribalism and identity politics are understandable sociological impulses, they are also factors that contribute to

43

our political division. Sustainable democracies require independence, compromise, and logic, which minimize knee-jerk reactions to different points of view. Tribalism and identity politics nudge us in the opposite direction and often manifest in prejudice, violence, and an overt hatred of the "other." "Succumbing to the all-too-human urge to hate for the sake of hating," and "to belong for the sake of belonging" pits us against each other and undermines our ability to self-govern.[6]

Both impulses also run counter to the apostle Paul's admonition to be "all things to all people" (1 Corinthians 9:22). Paul wrote his letter to the Galatians in direct response to the church's devolution into—you guessed it—identity politics and tribalism. While he was traveling, word came to him that church leaders were attempting to divide believers along racial and ethnic lines. In response, Paul commanded them to set aside man-made distinctions that would ultimately divide them: "There is neither Jew nor Gentile, neither slave nor free, nor is there male and female, for [we] are all one in Christ Jesus" (Galatians 3:28). This message reminded them of their true identities as family members in Christ. Getting that point across was so important to Paul that scholars tell us he grabbed his scribe's pen and wrote these words himself in huge letters (think ALL CAPS).

To be clear, Paul wasn't saying that distinctions between people shouldn't exist. Nor was Paul encouraging us to conform to other people's perspectives. Rather, Paul urges us to *choose* unity *in spite of our differences*—not because our differences are minor or insignificant, but because our commonalities in Christ are much greater.

When politics are at play, this truth is easy to forget. Christians are as guilty as everyone else of leading with their political affiliations rather than their affiliation with Christ. In some Christian circles, political conversations are even used to facilitate virtue signaling—a modern-day Pharisee's dream come true. Believers on both sides of the aisle have become so en-amored with the notion of ideological purity that we compete to see who can be the most conservative or socially conscious. And by doing so, we prioritize things of this world over that which is eternal.

## Reality Check

Given how easy it is to lose sight of these truths, it's critical that I remind *myself* of who I really am. Doing so keeps me grounded in self-love and helps me humanize those on the other side of an issue. Reminding myself that they, too, are beloved children of God enables me to value and honor them, regardless of how different our perspectives are. For that reason, I keep the following list of biblical truths on hand.

**I am royalty.** First John 3:1 marvels at this revelation: "See what great love the Father has lavished on us, that we should be called children of God! And that is what we are!" As a daughter of the King, I have royal blood coursing through my veins. Reminding myself of this truth helps me keep it classy, since I'm constantly asking myself, "Is *that* how a princess would respond?" This question helps to reorient my thoughts, words, and actions to mindsets, speech, and behavior that match my spiritual identity. It also infuses me with confidence and dignity, which help me treat others the way a true princess should.

**I am God's co-laborer.** In his first letter to the church at Corinth, the apostle Paul tells us that we each play different roles in bringing kingdom work into fruition. There is "one who plants" and "one who waters," but only God can make things grow. As such, we are all "co-workers in God's service" (3:7, 9).

The primary focus of our co-laboring with Christ is sharing the gospel and loving others. Keeping this mission front and center helps me stay focused on the spiritual purpose of my earthly work. It also reminds me that God cares far more about our eternal destinies than our political realities. This realization helps me stay focused on doing His will, in His way, rather than lone-rangering for causes that pale in comparison.

**I am a saint.** "I'm not perfect, just forgiven" used to be my go-to excuse whenever I sinned. For much of my life, I harbored this defeatist mindset rooted in religious doctrines that emphasized my fallen state as a sinner rather than my victorious reality as a saint.

The truth is, we're all natural-born sinners, and we all sin throughout our lives. Accepting Jesus as our Lord and Savior, however, means that the Holy Spirit now lives inside of us. Thus, we cannot possibly be the same people that we were before we met Christ. As the apostle Paul wrote, "If anyone is in Christ, the new creation has come: The old has gone, the new is here!" (2 Corinthians 5:17). This newness that Paul refers to is our spiritual transformation from sinner to saint.

Knowing that I'm a saint completely changes the way I think and engage with the world around me. I feel a new love and compassion toward friend and foe alike. The things I once loved, I now detest. The sin I once held on to, I now run from. In the words of Paul, I "have taken off [my] old self with its practices" (Colossians 3:9), and "put on the new self, created to be like God in true righteousness and holiness" (Ephesians 4:24). This self-awareness of my true identity changes everything about how I behave and view the world, including how I show up and engage in politics.

**I have a sound mind.** Second Timothy 1:7 says that "God has not given us a spirit of fear, but of power and of love and of a sound mind" (NKJV). This is a go-to verse for me that I repeat whenever I feel like I'm about to fly off the handle. It reminds me that emotional regulation and self-control are possible with God's help. It also reminds me that when I'm reacting in fear, that feeling isn't from God, and I have the power to overcome it with prayer and faith.

**I am brave.** This theme is sprinkled liberally throughout the Bible but quoted most often in Joshua 1:9, which reads, "Be strong and courageous." Politics isn't for the faint of heart. Opposition comes against anyone who has the courage to stand for truth. And everyone who's ever engaged in a political battle is bound to feel weak and overwhelmed at times.

That's why this reminder bears repeating: I am not how I *feel* in a moment of weakness; rather, I *am* strong and courageous, no matter how I feel. God is with me, and He is my strength. Keeping this truth at the forefront of my mind helps me *act* courageously, even when I feel like I'm anything *but*.

**I am a peacemaker.** Matthew 5:9 reads, "Blessed are the peacemakers," which makes me think that there aren't that many of us out there. Singling out peacemakers speaks to just how difficult it is to overcome our own pettiness, pride, and anger.

But becoming a peacemaker, while difficult, is a worthy and godly endeavor. Jesus sends us into a world that is filled with anger and violence to usher in His peace and love. The peace we carry distinguishes us from those who choose hatred and division instead. But, unfortunately, when some Christians (including me) engage in the realm of politics, we sometimes end up looking less like Jesus and more like the world around us. Rather than defusing a volatile situation, we often add fuel to the fire, which robs us and others of experiencing God's peace.

That's why it's so important that we consciously choose to lead with peace in politics. By being carriers of His shalom, we can help bring order to chaos, restore sanity and reason, and use disagreements as a means of expressing God's love toward everyone, including those with whom we disagree.

**I am capable.** NBA legend Stephen Curry and I share two things in common: our love of basketball and our obsession with Philippians 4:13, which reads, "I can do all things through Christ who strengthens me" (NKJV). Steph writes this verse on the side of his basketball shoes to remind him to reach higher and push harder in every practice and game. I type it in the manuscript of this book to remind myself that God can do miraculous things through me when my heart and mind are submitted to Him.

Self-confidence is an illusion that hinges on how we feel about ourselves at any given moment. Confidence in God, on the other hand, aligns our capabilities with His, which are limitless. Whenever I read this verse, I emphasize the word *all*—I can do *ALL* things through Christ who strengthens me. That means I *can* love those who hate me, forgive those who persecute me, and bless those who curse me because Jesus empowers me to (see Luke 6:27–28). This realization robs me of any excuse for treating those I disagree with differently. It also causes me to rely on God to do the hard work of loving my enemies.

**I am loved.** John 3:16 says that God loved us so much that He sent His only begotten Son to die for us. Romans 8:38–39 tells us that "neither death nor life, neither angels nor demons, neither the present nor the future, nor any powers, neither height nor depth, nor anything else in all creation, will be able to separate us from the love of God." Psalm 5:12 says that God surrounds us with his shield of love." Psalm 36 reminds us that God's love is "unfailing" (v. 7). And in Ephesians 3:18, Paul expresses his hopes that we might understand "how wide and long and high and deep is the love of Christ."

Love is our most basic human need, which is why God uses all of Scripture to remind us of His love for us. By experiencing His love personally, we're able to love others, including those we consider particularly disagreeable. Love transcends mere tolerance and enables us to extend His grace to others, regardless of how extreme their political positions seem. Love is also incredibly persuasive; God draws us into a relationship with Him because He first loved us. Loving others increases our political influence as well as the capacity of our hearts. The adage, it turns out, is true—whether in life, in work, or in politics, love always wins.

## REFLECTION

1. What labels have you internalized that are contrary to your God-given identity?
2. How have those labels affected your ability to show honor, love, and empathy toward those who sit on the other side of the political aisle?
3. What can you do to stay rooted in your true identity in Christ?

## PRAYER

*God, I realize how faulty my thinking is regarding my own identity, and I thank you that I am who you say I am. Change any false beliefs I cling to so that I can be empowered to act in a manner that reflects your love—not only toward those I agree with, but also toward my political "enemies." Change my understanding of others' identities by helping me see them through your eyes. Transform the way I show up in politics to reflect who I am in light of your love. In Jesus' name, Amen.*

# 3

# AMBASSADORS OF HEAVEN

The Christian is a man of heaven temporarily living on earth.

—A.W. Tozer

There's a legitimate reason why politics is a taboo dinner topic: it forces people to pick a side, which can ruin even the most delicious meal. Some of the godliest people I know struggle to keep a cool head when politics are broached. I've personally witnessed well-churched people go from zero to unhinged in the time that elapses between blessing their food and taking their first bite of Thanksgiving turkey. Only politics can set us off that quickly and irrationally.

Nevertheless, Christians are empowered to love and honor people, no matter how strongly we feel about an issue. How we treat others—whether we encourage them with hope, truth, and joy or discourage them with fear, lies, and shame—matters to God. As the Bible says, we are heaven's ambassadors, commissioned to reflect His love at all times (2 Corinthians 5:20).

And in the world of politics, our mission remains the same, both in and out of election season.

## Campaigning as an Ambassador

When I first joined Governor George W. Bush's campaign as a twenty-two-year-old, I gave very little thought to how my words and actions reflected on his candidacy. Sure, I'd learned to be a good witness for *Jesus*, but I'd never equated that to representing a *candidate* well. It never occurred to me that anything I said or did to get him elected could reflect poorly on the governor and have the opposite of my intended effect.

But one afternoon at a staff meeting, I realized just how wrong my thinking was on the matter. At the start of the meeting, our campaign manager asked an intern to step forward. He did so sheepishly, knowing he was about to be reprimanded for using his "Bush for President" credentials to score a reservation at a local restaurant. A friend of the governor saw him do it and reported him to the campaign. It was clear to everyone watching that this intern hadn't considered the ramifications of his actions. But the deed had been done, and now he had to suffer the consequences. By acting that way, he'd misrepresented the Governor's heart, which was to serve rather than be served. And in that moment, I realized that at all times and in all settings, I too was an ambassador of our campaign and candidate.

This awareness grew exponentially when I became the candidate. Since I was constantly in the spotlight, I grew keenly aware of how I acted and spoke in every setting. No matter how disrespectfully my opponents treated me, I did my best to respond to them with honor and love. As a candidate and a Christian, I represented my own political values as well as my faith.

In spite of my self-awareness, I failed from time to time—and epically at that. One such instance occurred when my opponent hired a tracker to stalk me. For ten solid months, a dude with a video camera followed me everywhere I went. He was large, bespeckled, and creepy. He rarely said a word and was always within six feet of me and anyone I spoke to. His goal was to irritate me so much that I'd eventually lash out at him, which he, in turn, would capture on camera and give to my opponent. For that reason, and no other, I determined to never melt down on film.

The first time my tracker showed up at a fundraiser, I tried treating him the way I thought Jesus would have. I offered him food and drink, spoke to him kindly, and protected him from my supporters, who were not happy that he was there. He accepted all of my hospitality; however, he was nothing but rude in return. Any time I spoke to him, he shoved his camera right in front of my face. At campaign events, he harassed constituents who didn't want to be filmed. And on and off for a solid month, he took up residence in our campaign headquarters.

In a matter of weeks, my resolve to be Christlike completely disappeared. The tipping point came when I caught him filming me through the window of my car. I'd had a difficult day and sought solace in what I thought would be a private place to cry. But my car was still fair game to him, so when I saw his camera pressed against my window, I lost my ever-loving mind. I jumped out of the car, screamed all sorts of obscenities, and grabbed his camera, intending to throw it to the ground. He laughed and said, "I knew I'd get to you eventually." At that, I froze, realizing I had no choice but to return his camera and walk away. The last thing I wanted was to be sued for battery in the middle of my campaign.

For days, I dwelled on the nasty things I'd said to him in the heat of the moment—things I'd never repeat aloud, especially in church. I fretted about the damage that video footage could do—how it would destroy my reputation as well as my witness. I'd been vocal about my faith from the moment I announced my candidacy, and people paid attention to everything I did and said. The last thing I wanted was to be—or be perceived as—yet another hypocrite.

What I *didn't* consider, until much later, was the impact my response may have had on my *tracker*—a living, breathing human being whom Jesus loved, in spite of his poor vocational choice. Being on the campaign trail, and wholly consumed with winning, caused me to view him through my own selfish lens. So while Missionary Denise would have gone out of her way to love on this guy, Candidate Denise saw him as a threat that needed to be eliminated.

Thankfully, God straightened my thinking out and taught me important spiritual lessons in the process. First, that my obsession with winning made me focused on earthly issues rather than heavenly matters. Instead of loving others, I was more focused on winning, often at others' expense. Second, by labeling my tracker an "enemy," I'd dehumanized him and made it easier to justify treating him poorly. It's easy to think that "enemies" get what they deserve, when God's children always deserve better. Third, just because my tracker worked for my opponent didn't give me license to treat him like a second-class citizen. Being on the "right" side of an issue never actually does.

## Lessons from the Campaign Trail

Over time, I've boiled these three lessons down into one: ends cannot *ever* justify means. Jesus loved my tracker and commanded me to do the same. It didn't matter that what I was trying to achieve was "for the glory of God." My tracker had innate worth that God wanted me to honor, regardless of his actions or beliefs. To God, loving my tracker was more important than pursuing an outcome that He could achieve without my help.

Once this lesson sunk into my head, God started working on my heart. I realized that while I'd never yelled at anyone like that before, I had often screamed bloody murder at them in my mind. I care so deeply about being on the "right" side of politics that I often think dishonoring thoughts about those I disagree with. Previously, I'd applauded myself for exercising self-restraint in keeping these thoughts inside, but this experience disabused me of such vanity. Even *thoughts* that dishonor God's children break His heart.

While I processed these truths, God asked me to repent, humble myself, and ask for my tracker's forgiveness. I *really* didn't want to, but I also realized that my representation of God's love was more important than any political ambitions I harbored. Eventually, I worked up the courage to apologize, which my tracker literally scoffed at. But since I wasn't doing it for him, per se, I wasn't overly concerned with his reaction. My apology stemmed from my obedience to God, which enabled me to be a better ambassador to those I met both on and off the campaign trail.

Through this ordeal, I learned the importance of integrity— acting the same way outside of church as I would in church. I never would have yelled at someone in my church parking lot, no matter how violated I felt. After all, Christians were watching (and judging)! But in that shopping center, in the heat of a campaign, popping off was my immediate reaction. I momentarily forgot that God was present, even if other witnesses weren't, and that my role as His ambassador extends to everyone, always.

These revelations reminded me of a sermon I'd heard years earlier titled "Ambassadors of Heaven." The preacher emphasized that the way we treat each other should reflect God's thoughts and feelings toward us. While I *knew* this to be true, knowledge alone hadn't positively impacted the way I acted toward, thought about, or treated people I disliked. Prior to listening to this sermon, my mind had erected a false sacred/secular division between godly and worldly things, with different codes of conduct for each. This preacher eviscerated such distinctions and taught me that being an ambassador for God in every aspect of my life was my highest purpose and calling.

## Earthly Ambassadors

Having worked in Washington, DC, and many world capitals, I've met and mingled with my fair share of ambassadors over the years. In the diplomatic realm, ambassadors are the highest-ranking envoys of their governments abroad. Their primary responsibilities are strengthening relations with host nations and advocating for their home countries' interests. Ambassadors have full authority to speak and act on their country's behalf. They also enjoy diplomatic immunity for their words and deeds whenever their code of conduct goes against their host countries' rules and laws. Ambassadors are subjects of their own countries, no matter where they live, and are judged and treated accordingly.

In my junior year of college, I spent a semester abroad, working at the British embassy in Beijing. One of the many perks of my internship was riding in the embassy's Rolls-Royce with the ambassador. Since I'd never met an ambassador before (nor ridden in a Rolls-Royce, for that matter), I used these opportunities to observe everything he did. Though an American, and just a lowly intern, I was cognizant of the fact that I represented the UK and the ambassador before the Chinese government. Emulating his mannerisms would ensure that I did things right.

Being British, the ambassador was exceedingly proper and polite. He exuded a quiet confidence in his identity as a representative of a powerful nation and never usurped his nation's interests with his own. Since he lived in China, he became well-versed in Chinese culture, spoke excellent Mandarin, and had many Chinese friends. In fact, if you closed your eyes and listened to him speak, you'd never know he wasn't a native speaker. But no matter how seamlessly he blended into Beijing's diplomatic scene, there was no mistaking who he represented or where his loyalties lay.

I learned a great deal from the ambassador about what it means to represent my God in politics, and in any other cultural sphere I find myself in. Ambassadors epitomize Scripture's instruction to be "*in* the world, but not *of* it" (John 15:19; 17:14–16). So when I heard the sermon, I drew immediate parallels between what I'd witnessed in China and how God expects me to represent Him on this side of heaven. As it turns out, God was preparing me to be His ambassador long before I entered the wild world of politics.

## Citizens of Heaven

In Philippians 3:20, the apostle Paul reminds us that "our citizenship is in heaven." Citizenship is a prerequisite for becoming an ambassador because citizenship determines our identity and our loyalties.

Both of my parents are naturalized immigrants, so American citizenship is something I consider to be sacred. My mother moved to the United States in 1969, after spending the first thirty years of her life in China and Taiwan. She knew almost nothing about American culture and spoke very little English but desperately wanted to embrace her adoptive country. From taking English classes, to launching an "American" career, to making American friends, to attempting to eat cheese (something only Asians can truly appreciate), my mom was all in from the moment she stepped foot on US soil.

My father was born and raised in Canada and moved to the United States with his family in high school. He loved America so much that he enlisted in the US Air Force at the age of seventeen to expedite his naturalization process. After serving twenty years in the military, my father continued his public service as a teacher and remains civically engaged to this day.

My parents are both still very proud of their native countries. They speak with accents reflecting their origins, prefer eating their childhood delicacies, and enjoy visiting their hometowns regularly. My parents still fly Canadian and Taiwanese flags at home, right beneath the American flag. And both still refer to themselves as Canadian and Chinese when asked where they are from. But both have also fully assumed their identities as Americans and take seriously their oaths of citizenship:

> I hereby declare, on oath, that I absolutely and entirely renounce and abjure all allegiance and fidelity to any foreign prince, potentate, state, or sovereignty, of whom or which I have heretofore been a subject or citizen.[1]

This oath, which they and millions of others have sworn, invokes mutual exclusivity. In pledging their loyalty to America, my parents chose to renounce their loyalties to the countries they grew up in. They understood that there are no "halfsies" when it comes to pledging allegiance; you're either all in or all out. Anything less than "all in" is tantamount to lying under oath.

Just as my parents changed their citizenship to American the moment they took their oaths, Christians become citizens of heaven the moment we accept Jesus as our Lord and Savior. Unlike the American citizenship process, which is long and arduous, heavenly citizenship is instantaneous. However, the rights and responsibilities of citizenship are the same in heaven as they are on earth: in choosing Jesus, we "renounce and abjure" our allegiance to all else.

## Undivided Loyalty

Just as all naturalized citizens swear oaths of allegiance to the United States, all appointed and elected officials, including ambassadors, must do the same.

> I, _____, do solemnly swear that I will support and defend the Constitution of the United States against all enemies, foreign and domestic; that I will bear true faith and allegiance to the same; that I take this obligation freely, without any mental reservation or purpose of evasion; and that I will well and faithfully discharge the duties of the office on which I am about to enter. So help me God.[2]

I still remember placing my left hand on the Bible and raising my right as I took this oath prior to starting my job at the White House. I felt the weight of every word and understood precisely where my loyalties would lie: no longer with the occupant of the Oval Office, but with my country and the Constitution.

God requires the same loyalty of us when we choose to follow Him. Putting God first requires us to put everything else—family, career, and our very selves—second. As applied to politics, that means putting human leaders, party platforms, and even our opinions *second* to representing His priorities, agendas, and truth.

There's simply no way to straddle both the world's way of doing things and God's—trust me, I've tried. As the Bible says, "No one can serve two masters, for either he will hate the one and love the other, or he will be devoted to the one and despise the other" (Matthew 6:24 ESV). While Jesus' teaching in that context was about money, one could substitute *politics* for *money*, and it would still be equally true. The apostle Paul takes this principle a step further in the book of Galatians, writing, "If I were still trying to please people, I would not be a servant of Christ" (Galatians 1:10). The choice between the two is mutually exclusive; we can either choose earthly things—political parties, patriotic identities, and politicians—or we can pledge our allegiance to God.

## Clear Agenda

A third requirement of ambassadorship is knowing and representing the priorities and policies of one's homeland clearly and consistently.

In order to protect and promote their homeland's interests abroad, earthly ambassadors must have a clear understanding of what their foreign policy objectives are. Knowledge, however, is only half the battle. Committing to uphold these policies is just as important as knowing what they are.

A semi-committed, half-knowledgeable ambassador is no ambassador at all. Unclear and inconsistent representation invariably results in diplomatic failure. As ambassadors of heaven, we cannot allow such confusion to obfuscate God's agenda on earth. Instead, we must stand for His truth in a manner that reflects His nature, regardless of how we feel about doing so.

I really struggled with applying this principle in the first few months of my campaign because I didn't ask God to clarify hot-button issues that were "gray areas" in the Bible. I resisted asking in part because I was torn between wanting to appeal to voters and wanting to represent biblical truth. For months, I struggled to come to terms with what my positions should be regarding these issues. However, straddling this line made me feel like such a charlatan that I eventually asked God for both clarification and the courage to represent His principles well, regardless of the political consequences it posed to my campaign. The moment I did, He gave me the conviction I needed to address these issues head on, and I became a more effective ambassador and politician for Him.

I share this story because I know how hard it is to represent God in a culture that doesn't abide by His laws. It's much easier to go with the flow, especially when swimming upstream is misinterpreted as being intolerant by culture, or a sellout by the church. But whether you're embraced or rejected, representing God at any cost is the price of discipleship. As Dietrich Bonhoeffer wrote, "When Christ calls a man, he bids him come and die."[3] In the context of politics, that means dying to any platform, policy, or way of engaging in politics that misrepresents heaven.

## Cultural Representative

Another requirement of ambassadorship is being a cultural representative abroad. As cultural liaisons, ambassadors reflect the nature and character of their homeland, whether they're engaged in official business at the office or personal errands around town. An ambassador may be the only representative of a country that their host nation ever sees. As such, everything they do—from how they speak to how they conduct themselves—determines how the nation they represent is perceived.

The weight of this responsibility is significant. Ambassadors must be circumspect in their words and activities and appealing in their mannerisms and behaviors. The success or failure of a diplomatic mission often rests on how well they are regarded by their host countries. This reality gives them even greater power to shape the success or failure of their diplomatic missions than their titles alone confer.

As a young, broke twenty-something, I attended many free parties on Embassy Row in Washington, DC. This neighborhood of our nation's capital is one of the most beautiful parts of the city, since it's where every nation puts its best foot forward. The embassy buildings are well maintained and appointed, their diplomats polished and polite, and the food and drinks the best of their nations' cuisines. Every reception I attended offered a glimpse into a country and culture that I could have otherwise gleaned only from traveling there myself.

Prior to attending their parties, I knew little to nothing about some of the countries that were represented on Embassy Row. After experiencing their hospitality, however, I was inspired to learn even more, finding myself favorably inclined toward nations I'd never even heard of. Their ambassadors successfully converted me from a hungry, clueless interloper into a curious, well-fed admirer by virtue of their gracious hospitality and positive representation of their own countries.

Imagine if, as ambassadors of heaven, we were as cognizant of reflecting the kingdom of God in the cultural realm of politics as the diplomats on Embassy Row are in Washington, DC. Imagine if we were as intentional about putting our best foot forward, treating others with honor and respect, and giving them a taste of God's love for them. Imagine if we were so committed to representing heaven well that we stood out among ambassadors of other worldviews and gods as the most gracious, welcoming, and hospitable people the world has ever encountered. Perceptions of us would change completely, and the favor we'd experience would be unparalleled.

Now take that perspective and apply it to politics. Imagine if every word we spoke represented God's life-giving truth. Imagine if our words and actions reflected God's nature and love—not only to our political allies, but also to our political enemies. Imagine if our demeanor was so welcoming that we drew those enemies to our doorstep with God's love, like bees to honey.

I know *exactly* what would happen if we took our roles as ambassadors as seriously as God wants us to. First, our generosity would help meet the physical and spiritual needs of the world. Second, our honoring words and actions would beckon the curious to learn more about Him. Third, we'd view ourselves differently—no longer as representatives of a party or platform, but as representatives of God. And fourth, we'd see others differently—not as enemies, but as children of God, whom we are commissioned by heaven to love.

## REFLECTION

1. Do you resonate more with your calling as an ambassador of heaven or as a member of a political party?
2. How does your chosen affiliation influence your behaviors?
3. What can you refrain from or initiate in your words, actions, or behaviors to better represent heaven in politics?

## PRAYER

*Father, thank you for reminding me of my true calling as an ambassador of heaven. Reveal all the ways in which my political activities and beliefs prevent me from reflecting who you are to a watching world. Bring my heart, mind, and actions into alignment with your standards for me. Help me be obedient to you in every situation, circumstance, and setting, so that I can be a blessing in the political realm and in every other sphere of culture I find myself in. In Jesus' name, Amen.*

# 4

# UNDISTRACTED

The most dangerous distractions are the ones you love, but that don't love you back.

—Warren Buffett

True confession: I'm a total news junkie.

My obsession kicks in early each morning as soon as my iPhone alarm goes off. While I wait the ten seconds it takes for my sleep data to update, my attention is invariably drawn to the Apple News app. As someone who struggles with FOMO, its lure is utterly irresistible.

It would be one thing if the obsession ended there, but it doesn't. Clicking on one link leads me to another, down a rabbit hole that I'd happily chase for hours if I could. The Apple News creators are no dummies; they embed their app with artificial intelligence and clickbait titles that are tailored to appeal to me. That's the only explanation I can come up with for how I start off reading the headlines du jour, and somehow end up reading articles titled, "10 things your dog needs RIGHT NOW."

What can I say? I'm a sucker for my golden retriever, and Apple News knows it.

While distractions are more prevalent than ever these days, they're an age-old problem. Every generation has been distracted by something or another, whether iPhones, books, or chipping away at a piece of flint for hours on end. More often than not, distractions start out as welcome breaks from the intensity of the real world. They can even be helpful in small brain-cleansing doses. But when distractions keep us from doing the things that matter most to God, they become problems that must be eliminated.

## Distraction v. Traction

Nerd alert: sometimes I study the etymology of words so that I can better understand their origins and meanings. While preparing to write this chapter, I studied the Latin origin of the word *distraction* and learned that *dis* means "apart or away," while *traction* is based on the word *trahere*, meaning "to drag." Putting the two together, distraction's literal meaning is "something that drags or pulls us apart or away" from what we *truly* desire by offering us instant gratification instead.

The opposite of distraction is traction. Traction moves us *toward*, rather than away from, what we really want. However, in order to move our lives in the right direction, we must first identify our true desires, which are rooted in our God-given purpose.

According to researchers, happiness lies in discovering our purpose.[1] According to Rick Warren, however, many of us miss our purpose and are thus unhappy, "because we typically begin at the wrong starting point—ourselves. We ask self-centered questions like What do *I* want to be? What should *I* do with *my* life? What are *my* goals, *my* ambitions, *my* dreams for *my* future?"[2] Questions like these are distracting because they focus us on our selfish ambition rather than our God-given purpose. Warren concludes in his bestselling book *The Purpose Driven*

*Life* that "without God, life has no purpose, and without purpose, life has no meaning. Without meaning, life has no significance or hope."[3] And without hope we cannot be happy.

Step one of living undistracted, therefore, requires determining our earthly calling and spiritual purpose. Early on, I realized mine was to be an advocate for justice and truth in politics. Beyond that, I hadn't given it much thought, which is why it took me years to connect my earthly calling (politics) with my spiritual purpose (loving God and others). This also explains why I often did politics "wrong"; instead of leading with my spiritual purpose, I led with my earthly calling, which caused me, and others, a great deal of angst. By flipping the two and putting my spiritual purpose first, I experienced greater success in my calling and more satisfaction in my purpose.

Identifying a distraction, however, can sometimes be tricky. That's because on its face, a distraction can sometimes look like traction. The difference between the two, psychologists say, lies in our intentions.

Take, for example, our careers. Since the Bible tells us to be excellent in our work (Colossians 3:23), working hard generally constitutes traction in the direction of our purpose and calling. However, when we allow work to replace other activities that are equally important—things such as relationships, leisure, and our physical and spiritual well-being—then work becomes a distraction, pulling us further away from, rather than in the direction of, our purpose.

When left unchecked, distractions can also take a turn for the dangerous. Engaging in distractions can often be much more fun than whatever else we were supposed to be doing at the moment. Consequently, distractions can serve as a cheap substitute for that which gives us true joy and meaning. And when we turn to them over and over again—out of season and out of control—distractions can turn into full-blown addictions, which rob us of our purpose and joy in life.

In the politically inclined, distractions can manifest through cable news outlets. For years, I watched Fox News from the moment I woke up until I fell asleep. Its reporters were my constant companions, and I even interviewed to work there myself. My devotion to Mr. Murdoch's empire further intensified when politically charged issues, like elections and wars, dominated headlines. Over the years, their "fair and balanced" reporting shaped my view of the world more than any other single influence, including Jesus.

For me, Fox News had all the hallmarks of an unhealthy distraction. First, it kept me from doing other important things, such as reading, working out, and socializing. Second, while it kept me well-informed, it generally did so through a lens devoid of biblical truths. Third, it highlighted differences between conservatives and liberals, making it harder for me to respect or engage with those on the other side of the aisle. So while watching Fox News helped me in my earthly calling, it actually kept me from my God-given purpose by making it harder for me to love those I disagreed with.

I know I'm not alone in struggling with this. I've listened to enough sermons lately to know that Christians are starting to wean themselves from obsessive news-watching. And lest anyone judge them otherwise, these aren't people who choose to be ignorant of what's happening in the world. Rather, they're God-honoring people who've realized that watching politically biased news distracts them from that which gives them true joy and meaning in life by influencing them to be more critical, divisive, and angry.

## Virtuous Distractions

Distractions are particularly sneaky when they present themselves as seemingly virtuous activities. In politics, distractions might look like skipping church or family events to volunteer for a righteous candidate or cause. For political staffers, spending late nights and weekends at the office can distract them from having necessary conversations at home. For candidates, a misplaced focus on beating "evil" opponents can usurp their responsibility to stand up for all that is right and good. And among civically engaged Christians, giving ourselves license to rail against "the swamp" prevents us from praying for leaders and the country we love.

Again, many who engage in such activities are well-meaning people who love God, America, and their fellow Americans. There's nothing inherently wrong or sinful in doing any of the activities listed above. But whether they serve as distractions from our God-given purpose hinges on our intentions in doing them. Are the things we're doing in the name of "righteousness" edifying ourselves and others? Or are they keeping us from fulfilling God's commandment to love because they fuel our need to be right? If our honest answers focus on the latter rather than the former, now's the time to eliminate such distractions from our lives.

It's also important to note that there's a season for everything. Those who are in a certain season need to go after whatever God has put on their hearts. Staying abreast of current events, while unhealthy in other contexts, was part of my job when I worked in the White House. Similarly, working around the clock to earn every last vote was part of my calling when I ran for Congress. Actions that would have qualified as distractions in any other context produced necessary traction in my life when they were taken for the right reasons, with the right heart, and at the right time. Again, it all boils down to our intentions, which only God and we can discern.

## Living Undistracted

Spiritual gurus have popularized the notion of living an undistracted life. Most, however, focus on achievement as their end goal, while Jesus prioritizes that which matters most to God. Christians are called to focus on more than just winning in life and in politics. Rather, we are urged to be consumed with living like Jesus did—in obedience, sacrifice, and love, with our hearts fixed on eternity. As Jesus wisely noted, it does no good for someone to gain the whole world (or win every election) but lose their soul in the process (Mark 8:36).

As a lover of God, I'd be miserable working in politics if winning was all I cared about. Obviously, the point of engaging in any campaign is to win, and not lose. But God cares as much, if not more, about *how* I go about winning than whether I actually win—the outcome of which ultimately lies in His hands. And if winning requires me to do things that distract me from my spiritual purpose, then I must risk losing in order to prioritize that which matters most to Him.

I realize this all sounds aspirational and hard to practically apply. So here are a few ways I've learned to maintain my traction with God while fully engaging in the political process.

**Identify your dual purposes in life.** For years, I prioritized my earthly calling over anything remotely spiritual. Consequently, I spent most of my twenties obsessing over what I was put on this earth to *do*. With laser-like intensity, I cultivated my vocational toolbox so that I could help catalyze the political change I wanted to see in America.

But by the age of thirty, I'd checked all the boxes that were on my list of career aspirations. That's when I realized there had to be more to life than merely achieving goals. While knowing our earthly purpose is important to God, that's only half the battle. The other half is knowing who we're created to *be*.

So I started asking God to illuminate the spiritual purpose of my life. As I did, the answer became clear: to make His love known to others by making His influence on my life evident in everything I said and did. When I live a life that's rooted in Him, it's easier both to love others and to fulfill my earthly calling. There's nothing more gratifying than loving what you do and doing it for people that you love.

I truly believe that identifying our dual purposes in life is the key to our happiness and fulfillment. As bestselling author Jack Canfield observed, "If you can tune into your purpose and really align with it . . . life flows much more easily."[4]

**Eliminate distractions.** Distractions are everywhere, all the time. In the same way that bakeries seem to be on every street corner when I'm committed to dieting, distractions are even more prevalent when I'm focused on God's priorities. This phenomenon is known as "the law of reverse effect"—the harder I try to focus, the more distractions I encounter.

There's obviously a spiritual element to this phenomenon as well. Christians characterize good and evil as evidence of God and the devil. The Bible says that the devil "walks about like a roaring lion, looking for someone to devour" (1 Peter 5:8). His primary goal is to steal, kill, and destroy those who love and obey God (John 10:10). Therefore, when we focus on doing things God's way, the devil is bound to kick the law of reverse effect into high gear. He does so by placing as many obstacles as possible between us and our God-given purpose.

Distraction is at the heart of the devil's playbook. We fight back by proactively eliminating any distractions we have control over. Like clearing a pantry of cookies before starting a new diet, we must rid ourselves of any influences that could derail us from our purpose. In the area of politics, that could mean taking a break from social media or, as in my case, minimizing cable news consumption. Distractions are easily overcome when we know what they are. So focus on identifying yours, and commit to eliminating them up front.

**Set up guardrails.** I first heard about the concept of guardrails from one of my favorite pastors, Andy Stanley. Guardrails, he tells us, are systems "designed to keep vehicles from straying . . . into dangerous or off-limit areas."[5] They're strategically placed a few feet before a driver enters an actual danger zone, so that hitting one causes a small accident that prevents a bigger one from happening.[6]

Similarly, spiritual guardrails establish a standard of behavior that trips our conscience when we wander into spiritual danger zones. They play the same role in our hearts as physical guardrails do by both protecting us from danger and keeping us on track. Just as we need physical guardrails to protect us in perilous parts of our journey, we need spiritual guardrails to keep us from veering off course with God—especially regarding our treatment of one another.

Relationships bear the biggest brunt of any division we allow to creep into our lives. That's why spiritual guardrails are so important for those who engage in politics. It's easy to justify trash-talking a party or candidate, all in the name of truth. But Scripture says to speak the truth *in love* (Ephesians 4:15), so one of the many guardrails I've instituted in politics is identifying myself as a Christian early in the conversation. Doing so holds me accountable for how I represent God in politics, and keeps me from making up my own rules of engagement as I go.

**Forgive.** Politicians are notorious for spending fourteen of their fifteen seconds of fame blaming their opponents for everything that's wrong with the world. And since we don't have all the facts ourselves, we tend to believe what we want. When all that we hear and see are criticisms and finger-pointing, it's hard to avoid falling into the same trap ourselves. And falling for that trap is what accounts for much of our political division today.

A cardinal rule of campaigning is to "go negative, early and often." I learned that in college and put it to work on the Bush campaign, attacking anyone who threatened our position as the party favorite. In South Carolina's all-important primary, we focused our attacks on Senator John McCain and his family. Our scorched-earth strategy worked, and we won South

Carolina by a landslide—but our victory came at a cost. Senator McCain was furious with then-Governor Bush, and their rift caused widespread dissension within Republican ranks.

I've gotta hand it to Senator McCain though; after nursing his wounds, he did a remarkable job of sweeping their differences under the rug—so much so that he earned President Bush's endorsement when he became the party's presidential nominee eight years later. By forgiving the president, Senator McCain succeeded in his own political endeavors. I'm sure it wasn't easy for him to move past what happened in that primary, but I'm glad he did. In the end, he united our party behind his nomination and was highly regarded for doing so.

Forgiving others is difficult, but never more so than when your character—and that of your loved ones—is under attack. I experienced this personally in my own campaign for Congress. My primary opponents characterized me as every unflattering thing you could imagine, while lying about my loyalties to our party and platform. A local reporter blatantly lied about everything I did and never retracted anything he wrote. Many in my own party refused to support me because I didn't endorse their chosen presidential candidate. But what hurt me most was the fact that some of my closest friends decided to support my opponent—some privately, others publicly.

At the beginning of my campaign, I took everything personally—it felt impossible not to. And since I'm more likely to fight than I am to cry, I grew bitter and tough. Like a squirrel gathering nuts for the winter, I hoarded my hatred for those who hated me. I tried not to show it because I didn't want my enemies to know how much they affected me, and because I didn't want to be outed as a bad Christian who hated her enemies. So I smiled on the outside—a fake, clenched grin—while inside, I burned with rage.

To be fair, unforgiveness is practically a Gitsham family virtue. As a child I was taught not to get mad, but to get even instead. I never started fights myself, but if someone started one with me, our whole family got involved. An eye for an eye was the name of our family game, and if I went down, we all went down swinging.

So even after I became a Christian, I struggled long and hard with bitterness and vengeance. It took years to undo my family's hard wiring, and decades to submit this part of my heart to God. To be honest, I still struggle to forgive—old habits die hard. But with practice and a whole lotta prayer, I'm learning to get better at it.

**Keep your eyes on your own paper.** The media has a million things to offer if you're looking for something to get mad about or someone else to blame. They make their money by keeping you glued to the television in outrage, paranoia, and fear. Good news is nice, but boring; bad news and gossip are titillating. If you need proof of this, just google which political commentators have the highest ratings—outrage is all the rage, especially in politics.

To that point, my best advice is "Don't believe the hype." Having worked in politics, I can promise you that no one is as good or bad as the media makes them out to be. Everything you read or watch is tainted by an opinioned human. The media never reports the full truth, so take everything you read with a grain of salt. Don't let what someone else says cloud your judgment or poison your soul.

Instead, embrace what's in *your* power to change. Forget what others are or are not doing; focus on what *you* can do to positively affect the world. Our lives, communities, families, and nation would be far better off if we spent more time engaging civically and less time complaining.

Distractions are inevitable in politics and life, and trying to minimize them can feel like playing a game of whack-a-mole. Thankfully, God has given us the upper hand over the devil and his schemes, so victory is ours for the choosing.

## REFLECTION

1. What distractions regularly derail you from your God-given purpose and calling?
2. What can you do to eliminate distractions that *are* within your control?
3. How can you eliminate distractions that *aren't* within your control?

## PRAYER

*Lord, I want to live a life that's fully aligned with your purpose and calling for me. Help me identify and eliminate any distractions that keep me from being able to do so. Thank you for your spiritual guardrails that keep me on track. May I rely on them less and less as I follow you more closely. In Jesus' name, Amen.*

# 5

# UNOFFENDED

Offense is an event, but offended is a decision.

—Steven Furtick

On a bright and sunny day in 2007, I backed my car out of a friend's driveway in San Francisco's Mission District and nearly hit a vehicle that sped past me on the street. The sunlight, which rarely appeared in that part of the city, blinded my bleary eyes, which were nearly crossed from late nights spent studying for the bar exam. The driver of the car stopped and backed up to confront me, so I rolled my window down to apologize. But as I sought to make eye contact, I realized he wasn't looking at my face; instead, he was fixated on my rear window, where a "Bush-Cheney 2000" bumper sticker was prominently displayed.

When he finally looked me in the eyes, I felt the full force of his wrath. "YOU! You're one of THEM!" he screamed as he let loose a tirade of anti-Bush epithets that would have made a sailor blush. My blood boiled, but I bit my tongue and waited for him to calm down before I tried engaging him in a more rational manner. Sadly, that didn't work—the more he yelled, the angrier he became, to the point where he actually got out of his car and strode toward me like he wanted to rumble. I took that as my cue to drive away. The last thing I wanted was a physical showdown on the streets of San Francisco, where I'd have no back-up for my Bush-loving self.

That wasn't the first time someone in our family had been threatened with physical violence over politics. My father had a similar experience in our otherwise congenial hometown during the 2004 presidential election. While waving campaign signs on busy street corners, he was regularly insulted and flipped off. None of that bothered him except on one occasion, when a guy took it a step further by stopping his car in the middle of our town's busiest intersection and walking toward my dad menacingly with a baseball bat in his hands. Thankfully, my father's prescience had led him to invite our family friend Rick to join him in the sign-waving that day. Rick was a fifth-degree black belt who stood six-foot-three-inches tall and weighed 240 pounds of pure muscle. After taking a look at Rick, the guy turned around and drove off, but I shudder to think what would have happened if Rick hadn't been there to protect my dad.

Sadly, these stories seem tame compared to the times we're living in today. Politically motivated violence has grown so commonplace that rather than being shocked by it, we *anticipate* it. In my friend circle alone, I've got a school board member who receives weekly threats and insults directed at her, her family, and their business; an attempt on the life of a prominent political donor by way of politically motivated arson; regular death threats directed at a US Senator, requiring him to double up on bodyguards and change his daily routine; and ongoing protests outside the home of a former boss, which caused him to pack his family up and move to another *state*. It seems everyone and everything related to politics is fair game these days, and we've somehow accepted violence as the price of doing business.

I know I'm not alone in thinking this, but it still needs to be said: as freedom-loving Americans, we must *stop* accepting hatred and violence as the price of our civic engagement. Physical violence is not protected speech under the First Amendment of our Constitution. Moreover, violence undermines democracy because it threatens our security as individuals and stability as a nation. If we love America and our way of life, we must stop letting differences in opinions devolve into physical manifestations of hatred.

Spiritually speaking, hatred and violence are rooted in a spirit of offense, which requires far more than pledges of mere tolerance to end. Tolerance is a nose-holding acceptance of those who believe, act, and think differently than us, requiring nothing more than peaceful coexistence to endure. Love, on the other hand, eclipses tolerance by ridding our hearts of offense and helping us view and treat others the way God intended.

Tolerance can coexist with offense, but love cannot. When push comes to shove, we must choose to either indulge in offense or rise above it. Rising above it, however, requires more than mere tolerance; it requires God-given grace and supernatural love.

### Sterne or Voltaire?

Thanks to Broadway, everyone knows about the infamous duel that ended Alexander Hamilton's life. As his namesake's musical so brilliantly portrays, Hamilton and Burr were at each other's throats for decades. Both had publicly thrown each other under the bus, with Hamilton stating that he felt a "religious duty" to oppose Burr's career. All of this was too much for Burr, who lost his gubernatorial election due to Hamilton's relentless attacks. So Burr challenged Hamilton to an "affair of honor"—the gentleman's term for a duel.

Back in their day, duels were often resolved before any bloodshed occurred. Hamilton, being the more outspoken of the two, had been involved in many such duels previously, and had resolved them all peaceably. Burr, however, was so offended that he refused to negotiate his way out of the duel. His spirit of offense was so strong that he was willing to risk his own life and reputation to avenge it.

No one knows if it happened in real life or not, but in the musical, both acknowledged that offense is a stupid reason to put their lives on the line. In the song "Ten Duel Commandments," Burr and Hamilton concur that "duels are dumb and immature."[1] Nevertheless, Burr chose to stay the course and follow through with the duel. So they each took shots at each other, and Hamilton died with Burr's bullet buried deep in his stomach. The country was so outraged that Burr was permanently relegated to persona non grata status. Offense thus led to the deaths of two men that day—one physically, the other reputationally.[2]

While Burr never expressed public remorse for his actions, historians tell us that he admitted he could have handled things differently in the latter years of his life. Speaking to his friends and family, Burr is recorded as saying, "Had I read Sterne more and Voltaire less, I should have known the world was wide enough for Hamilton and me."[3]

Sterne and Voltaire were popular European philosophers who had very different ways of expressing their political opinions. Voltaire wrote in "polarizing, succeed-or-die-trying" language, while Sterne was a clergyman who promoted acceptance and respect. Burr's admission—that he fed his offense by reading incendiary texts written by Voltaire—tells us a great deal about the importance of who we let influence our politicking.

Much has been said by both secular and religious commentators regarding the pervasiveness of offense today. But offense, as we all know, has been prevalent in the world for as long as people have roamed the earth. The Bible's first recorded murder, of Abel by his brother Cain, was spurred by offense. Cain was so offended at God's rejection of his sacrificial offering compared with His acceptance of Abel's, that he murdered Abel in a fit of jealousy and rage (Genesis 4:3–8). The rest of Scripture is filled with similar stories of angry people doing sinful things, all in the name of offense. Whether it manifests in murder, duels, or political outrage, the spirit of offense corrodes everything it touches.

## The Outrage Economy

Social commentators tell us that businesses today are capitalizing on our "outrage economy." Political anger has proven to be good for publicity, and businesses are tapping into it as well. As author Noah Rothman writes, "There is a thriving marketplace for outrage,"[4] the root of which lies in offense. This explains why corporations that don't have a conscience act as if they do. Their marketing teams tell them that if they adopt culture's outrage and double down on it, people will feel more aligned with their values and be more likely to buy their products. Thus, corporate America fuels the fire of offense, and we buy into it—both literally and figuratively.

This is true of the media as well, in that the more incendiary the content, the more likely it will be shared. Media sensationalism is nothing new, but mainstreaming offense is. It used to be said that sex sells. Nowadays, outrage does. So long as polarizing headlines capture eyeballs and increase ad revenues, reporters will keep on writing them. Commoditization of offense has become a legitimate part of the industry's marketing plan.

While it's easy to point fingers at business and media, it's harder to admit that we're all personally enamored with offense. We might not be the ones picking a fight, but we all like taking sides. Aligning with a team appeals to our human desire to belong to like-minded groups of people who validate our beliefs. And since there's always someone on the wrong side of that equation, there's always a plausible defense for feeling offended.

This is true of all people, regardless of their political, religious, or philosophical positions. Our desire to be right is rooted in the sin of pride, which is part of our fallen human nature. Pride has led to millions of relationship-ending events, from divorces to legal battles to wars. That's because pride, manifested in offense, is the most divisive force in the world.

Pride and offense are also the root causes of our nation's division today. They run rampant on both sides of the aisle; so much so that a "national divorce" between red and blue states was recently proposed by one politician.[5] And while most Americans reject this notion as utterly preposterous,[6] many of us carry it out in private by shunning those we disagree with politically in our personal and professional lives.

Politicians add fuel to the fires of our offense by framing every campaign as a zero-sum game. When leaders position each election as an existential crisis, the electorate believes that our very survival depends on "us" winning and "them" losing. This mentality prevents us from thinking critically about the policy decisions we support by putting us in survival mode rather than encouraging us to consider what's best for our nation and each other.

## Righteous v. Unrighteous Offense

Many have tried reconciling their human impulses and Christian faith by justifying their offense as "righteous." And sometimes, they're right. Consider slavery, 9/11, the slew of recent church and school shootings, and the ongoing abuses of power on Main Street, Wall Street, and Capitol Hill. All offer valid reasons to be offended and outraged. These violent, cruel, and abusive events and practices are patently wrong and evil. And anger is a natural response to them, born of our God-given desire for justice.

Jesus himself was offended when crafty businessmen tried profiting off those coming to Jerusalem to worship God at Passover. Incensed, "Jesus made a whip from some ropes and chased them all out of the Temple. He drove out the sheep and cattle, scattered the money changers' coins over the floor, and turned over their tables. Then, going over to the people who sold doves, he told them 'Get these things out of here. Stop turning my Father's house into a marketplace!" (John 2:13–16). Jesus was furious at those who took advantage of worshipers by selling them overpriced animals and engaging in price-gouging currency exchanges. But His anger wasn't caused by His own pride or a feeling of personal offense. Rather, He was righteously offended by the corruption and injustice that hurt *other* people.

Lest we use this example to justify our own offended sensibilities, there are a few nuances worth considering. For one, Jesus was innocent in a way that none of us are. As natural-born sinners, our hands are not clean. Therefore, it behooves us to engage in some level of prayerful introspection as to our own offensive behaviors before declaring ourselves "justifiably righteous" in our anger.

Offense is almost always triggered by the pride of thinking that our hearts, minds, and actions are above those of another. Saying (or thinking), "I would *never* do something like that!" is just one indication of our own pride. When we recognize that we are often just as guilty as anyone else, it's a lot harder to be offended by their actions. We can correct them. We can point out their sin. We can even try to stop whatever they're doing.

But offense is much harder to justify when we acknowledge the true state of our own hearts.

Another distinction to consider is whether we're offended on behalf of *others*, or because of how *we're* being treated ourselves. Scripture tells us that when Jesus was "reviled and insulted, He did not revile or insult in return; while suffering, He made no threats [of vengeance], but kept entrusting Himself to Him who judges fairly" (1 Peter 2:23 AMP). Jesus never took justice in His own hands, even though He had every right to do so. Rather, He trusted God to avenge every wrong committed against Him and asks us to do the same.

Jesus assured His disciples that in this life, "offenses will certainly come" (Luke 17:1 CSB). And boy, was He right! Our culture is teeming with offense, and nowhere more so than in politics. His warning, however, lets us decide in advance how we'll respond when offenses do come. King Solomon, the wisest man who ever lived, wrote, "It is to one's glory to overlook an offense" (Proverbs 19:11). We'd be wiser still, and far happier, if we took his teaching to heart.

## The Dangers of Taking Offense

Being offended is so normalized in our culture that we rarely recognize the danger it poses to our souls. Yet *offense* is actually a translation of the Greek word *skandalon*, which means "trap" or "snare." Traps are laid in the well-worn paths of their intended victims to catch them while they're going about their normal routines. They draw us in with something we want while blending seamlessly into our surroundings.

Similarly, offense lures us with the temptation of reacting to something that strikes us as being outrageous. Like an animal feasting on bait, we hardly notice we're even trapped, since everyone around us seems to share the same offended mindset. This is especially true of political offense: the bait of self-righteousness or desire for vindication are so great, and offense so commonplace, that we happily grab hold of what we want without even realizing we've been caught. It takes Holy Spirit discernment and conviction to help us realize that we've been ensnared.

As Scripture says, offense is inevitable. In politics, it's embedded in every headline, speech, and bumper sticker. But avoiding it to the extent we're able to, and asking God to protect our hearts from it when we aren't, should be a priority for every Christian for the following reasons.

**Offense is self-perpetuating.** Once trapped, we're told a number of lies that keep us addicted to feeling offended. The most tempting one to believe is that expressing anger alleviates our pain and frustration. You hear this a lot in our current political climate, which encourages people to "let it all out" and "speak their truth"—as if adding more outrage to the conversation has the power to resolve things or make us feel any better.

Psychologists have discovered that the *opposite* is true. Acting on our outrage only makes us *more* outraged, not less. When people vent their feelings, their blood pressure spikes, and they end up making themselves angrier.[7] Catharsis, it turns out, is a "total flop" in terms of fixing a situation or making us feel better about it.[8] So do yourself a favor and avoid offense—for your own sake as well as others'.

**Offense victimizes us.** The spirit of offense rears its ugly head whenever we feel victimized by someone else's actions or words. We fall prey to a victim mentality when we:

☑ See ourselves as being powerless in a situation where we actually have resources and options to do more than we are doing,

☑ See ourselves as innocent parties on the receiving end of someone else's misbehavior without recognizing our contribution to the struggle we're engaged in, and

☑ Develop an identity that is based on grievance and complaint, which may be partially true, but which also serves to define us through a sense of limitation, lack, and injustice.

As previously noted, victimization is a lie that flies in the face of everything God says we are. Scripture says that we are "more than conquerors," that we are "the head, not the tail," and that "no weapon formed against [us] shall prosper" (Romans 8:37; Deuteronomy 28:13; Isaiah 54:17 NKJV). We cannot be victims when the Bible says that we are victors, for "if God is for us, who can be against us?" (Romans 8:31).

**Offense undermines our credibility.** When we're perpetually offended, people eventually tune us out. Like the little boy who cried wolf, our outrage gets us the attention we want at first. But eventually, those who have the power to do something about it ignore us when they realize that we're operating with a distorted sense of reality.

The last thing we want to be known as is whiny, powerless people who see offense everywhere we look. Yes, there are horrible injustices in politics—things that utterly break God's heart and should break ours as well. But rather than complain about how they affect us, we should ask God how He can use us to fix them.

**Offense is divisive.** Everyone I know has had uncomfortable political encounters with family members that we can't tune out or cancel. Even my dad and I—both Republicans and conservatives—had it out one afternoon over a candidate he loved that I could not stand.

"They're going to ruin our country, and everything our party stands for!" I shouted. "You're crazy for contributing to their campaign!"

"I'd still choose them to run our country over you!" he replied, which really hurt my feelings, since I'd just lost my own race for Congress and was contemplating running again.

In a rare moment of offense, my father, who is also my biggest cheerleader, allowed his loyalty to an individual he didn't even know to come between the two of us. It would have been one thing if he'd said, "Honey, we're just going to have to agree to disagree on this one," which is what I usually get when we argue. But this was a candidate he was so loyal to that he was willing to drop an atom bomb on our relationship just to make a political point. And I, being the instigator, was guilty for picking the fight with him in the first place.

In moments like these we're all faced with a choice: do we respond in kind to the one who offended us, or forgive them and work on restoring the relationship? My answer was easy in that situation, both because I started it and because I love my dad more than life. It took a while for me to simmer down, but when I finally called to tell him how much his comments stung, he told me he hadn't even realized the impact of what he'd said. I'd offended him so deeply that his response was reflexive. We asked for each other's forgiveness and moved on with our lives, but the fact that our conversation went the way it did still surprises me to this day.

There aren't many people with whom forgiveness comes quite as readily as my father. Frankly, this is an aspect of my growth that still needs a lot of work. When I'm not emotionally connected to people, I can be quick to cut them off and allow offense to drive a permanent wedge between us. But God is working overtime to perfect me in this regard by urging me to revisit my offense, identify the trigger that caused me to react, and apologize to the other person for any role I played in bringing it about. I'm also learning to ask better questions of those who offend me. Curiosity can reward us with greater understanding and grace for offenses. I'm not always eager to reengage and reconcile with everyone He asks me to, but the positive difference it's making in my relationship with God and others is proving to be worth the effort.

## Overcoming Offense

I once read a *Dear Abby* column that stated, "A bad habit never disappears miraculously. It's an undo-it-yourself project." This quote reminded me that I am solely responsible for undoing that which sabotages my own growth and joy in life. Since offense robs me of both, it is a habit I'd like to undo. As such, I've listed a few of the steps below that help me move in that direction.

**Grow in self-awareness.** One of my fondest memories is being a student at Wellesley College in the spring of 1997. Wellesley is the alma mater of some of the most remarkable women in history. From Madeleine Albright to Hillary Clinton, and Madame Chiang Kai-shek to my cousin Susan, I'd always been in awe of those who'd graced her halls. When the opportunity to spend a semester there presented itself, I jumped at it.

I chose Wellesley over other colleges because I wanted to experience the thrill of sisterhood that my cousin Susan waxed poetic about. I was an only child who always wanted sisters, and Susan was as close as I got to the real deal. Her love of Wellesley and its tight-knit, all-female student body evoked a picture in my mind of a group of brilliant women walking around in sweats, encouraging each other to reach their full potential.

When I arrived, it was all I'd hoped it would be, and I felt like I'd died and gone to academic heaven. But I also learned that the sisterhood had a dark side that I was previously unaware of. Most of my classes were taught from a liberal feminist perspective, which was interesting, informative, and in many cases factual, but caused me to develop a low-level hatred of men. I had no idea how indoctrinated I was until I went on a mission trip with a co-ed group of peers that summer. When I noticed some distancing with one guy in particular, I asked him about it. "Denise," he replied, "I'm scared to say anything around you. You're dropping the chauvinist card left and right, and I feel like I'm being accused of something I'm not even guilty of."

His words hit me like a ton of bricks. I had no clue I'd been walking around with a chip on my shoulder. His words revealed how thoroughly ensnared I was by a doctrine that wasn't even mine. Once he flagged it for me, my sensitivity to this offense enabled me to separate fact from fiction, and I was better able to distinguish between actual and perceived gender-based slights. When it comes to overcoming offense, self-awareness is key.

**Be curious.** Three of my five closest girlfriends are Democrats, another's an Independent, and only one is a card-carrying Republican. This baffles the friends I've made in other states—especially those from California and Texas, where people tend to choose friends who think more like them. What they don't realize is that in a town like Washington, DC, where control alternates between parties every two years, you have to learn to get along with everyone. As the founder of my law firm always said, "Be nice to your interns—they'll likely be your boss some day!" The same is true of being nice to those across the aisle—if you don't know how to make bipartisan friends, your career in politics is doomed.

As a young politico, I quickly regressed into the mindset of a teenager: I thought that I was right and anyone I disagreed with was unequivocally wrong. But when I was forced to ask Democrats for their help after they took control of the White House and both chambers of Congress in 2008, I realized we were more alike than we were different. We all shared a common vision for a more equitable and just America. We all wanted our families and friends to achieve the American dream. And we all loved serving our country, which we'd all made personal sacrifices to do.

These realizations helped me not only enjoy working with Democrats, but *choose* to be their friend. Our friendships, in turn, gave me opportunities to ask sincere questions as to why they believed what they did. I was genuinely curious about their lives and experiences and learned that many of their positions were just as rational as mine. As my respect for them grew, so did the strength of our friendships.

Curiosity is sorely lacking in the political realm these days. Humility is a lost virtue that must be restored. You can't be curious if you think you know everything. That's why making friends with those who have different political perspectives, and really listening to what they believe in and why, is the most important step we can all take to help make politics less divisive, and a lot more fun.

**Cut off your supply.** Like Aaron Burr, we would all be well-advised to choose better spiritual and emotional inputs. As his duel with Hamilton proved, filling our minds with incendiary thoughts only hardens our hearts rather than softening them. That makes it more difficult to maintain an attitude of humility and stay grounded in love. We should guard our hearts from what poisons them—as much for our own spiritual and emotional health as our country's political well-being.

**Forgive.** Nelson Mandela is famously quoted as saying, "Resentment is like drinking poison and then hoping it will kill your enemies."[9] The reason this saying is so popular is that we've all had to remind ourselves of its truth. Forgiving people who've offended us is hard and grueling work. Nevertheless, it's required in order for us to experience spiritual, relational, and emotional growth.

Forgiveness is central to our faith, a doctrine founded on God's grace for those, like me, who repeatedly offend Him by flaunting His commandment to love others well. I have to remind myself daily of how great God's love is and how unmerited His mercy is toward me. This realization keeps my ego in check by reminding me of how much I have to be forgiven for. And when I dwell on my own need for His forgiveness, I find it harder to be offended by others.

**Be grateful.** The fastest way to kill a negative thought is to replace it with a grateful one. Gratitude is considered a spiritual practice by many and for good reason. Gratitude enriches our minds, bodies, and souls by bringing us into harmony with ourselves, with God, and with others. When we're in a posture of gratitude, there isn't room in our hearts for negativity. Gratitude makes us magnanimous and kind, making it difficult to find anything or anyone offensive at all.

Offense is an easy trap to fall into, and one that we all encounter in the political arena. But whether we succumb to its snare or sidestep it entirely is our choice alone. Scripture says that "the temptations in your life are no different from what others experience" and that God "will not allow the temptation to be more than you can stand." The verse continues, promising that when we are tempted, God "will show you a way out so that you can endure" (1 Corinthians 10:13 NLT). Reminding ourselves of these powerful truths helps us avoid taking the bait of offense in the first place. And thus, we can maintain our honor and love, regardless of the political atmosphere we live in.

## REFLECTION

1. On a scale of 1–10, how offended do you feel by what's happening in politics today?
2. What are you offended by, and why?
3. What behaviors and beliefs should you eliminate, and what habits should you adopt, to protect your heart from such offense in the future?

## PRAYER

*Lord, I admit that I am easily offended and struggle to forgive others the way you continuously forgive me. Search my heart and shine a light on any offense I'm holding on to. Free me from the trap of offense, and help me overcome it, so that it never again compromises my ability to love and honor those I disagree with. In Jesus' name, Amen.*

## 6

# INOFFENSIVE

When they go low, we go high.
—Michelle Obama

As a twenty-two-year-old on the Bush campaign, I was in constant awe of the famous people who came to visit my boss. From Michael Dell to Peggy Noonan, Condoleezza Rice to Ralph Reed, our visitor log boasted a who's who of the most influential people in the world.

One fall afternoon, a Christian leader I greatly admired came to visit us at campaign headquarters. I eagerly volunteered to escort him and could hardly contain my fangirling. I'd read this man's books, listened to his sermons, and held him in the highest regard. As I walked him back to my boss's office, I briefly considered asking for his autograph but decided that would be way too awkward. Instead, I listened in on his conversation with my boss—and what I heard shocked me.

The point of their meeting was to come up with a list of faith-based leaders who would publicly support Governor Bush's candidacy. This leader spoke glowingly about his recommendations and a few that my boss suggested they add. But for those he'd disagreed with—and especially for those who'd offended him publicly—he had harsh, damning, and judgmental words that went well beyond why they weren't a good fit and went straight to the merits of their character.

I couldn't believe my ears. This man who'd built his entire ministry on the principle of loving God and others was more concerned with avenging those who'd offended him than helping us figure out who would be a good fit for our campaign. Instead of turning the other cheek, he said offensive things about them, all within the confines of (thin) campaign office walls. To be fair: unflattering and cruel things had been spoken about him publicly by other Christian leaders. Nobody could accuse him of throwing the first punch, but he'd always held himself out as one who took the high road. That's one of the many reasons I was so disappointed by everything I heard him say.

We're all crushed when our heroes disappoint us, and it happens often because, like us, they're human. Whether in ministry, business, government, or entertainment, stories like these are more common than we wish they were. Even the most upstanding Christians are fallible when it comes to being offensive. It's a natural response to taking offense, which is not only pervasive but *encouraged*. Whether on the playground, on the playing field, or in the political realm, everyone seems to love a good old-fashioned fight.

Everyone, that is, but Jesus.

## Offense Is Dangerous

In Luke 17, Jesus teaches His disciples how to respond to those who sin against them. "Offenses will certainly come," He says, "but woe to the one through whom they come!" (Luke 17:1

csb). In this verse, Jesus acknowledges the fact that we live in a fallen world, where offense is inevitable. But being *offensive* is both unacceptable and dangerous for those who've chosen to follow Him. To make that point extra clear, Jesus throws in a warning: "Watch yourselves!" (Luke 17:3 NLT).

Duly noted, and yet so hard to do. Our culture, like the one Jesus lived in, considered being offensive a justifiable reaction to offense. If it hadn't, Jesus wouldn't have delivered this "eye for an eye" rebuttal in the Sermon on the Mount:

> Do not resist the one who is evil. But if anyone slaps you on the right cheek, turn to him the other also. And if anyone would sue you and take your tunic, let him have your cloak as well. And if anyone forces you to go one mile, go with him two miles.
>
> Matthew 5:39–41 ESV

In these verses, Jesus turned the cultural and religious teachings of their day and ours upside down. A slap means the same thing today as it did back then—and didn't necessarily involve literal, physical violence. Rather, a slap referred to any offensive personal slight. As we all know, a metaphorical "slap in the face" can be just as offensive as a physical slap and equally damaging to our pride. So imagine being asked by Jesus to endure not one, but two!

Similarly, in a time when tunics were hard to come by and most people had just one, giving someone both your tunic *and* your cloak would have been tantamount to giving them your entire wardrobe. That's a lot to ask of *anyone*, much less someone offended by the greedy person asking. In this era, Roman soldiers were legally capable of requiring anyone they asked to carry all of their belongings for up to a mile. Everyone hated that law—hence His use of the word *force*—and here we have Jesus asking us to endure not one, but two miles of being a Roman soldier's packhorse.

Jesus used these examples to set a new standard of behavior for His followers, which flipped the script on culture. Rather than condone offense in return for offense, Jesus commands us to be *inoffensive*, not by skirting around hard truths or becoming Christian doormats, but by *loving* those who offend us. Ironically, doing so gives us the upper hand over our enemies because it preserves our peace and prevents us from sinning. And it can actually make those we show unmerited grace toward hate us even more, since our loving response highlights the depravity of their own words and ways.

Of course, this was all too much for the Jewish leaders who had prayed for a Messiah that would deliver them *from,* rather than instruct them to remain *under,* oppressive Roman rule. So they were understandably upset at Jesus' suggestion that they not only *submit*, but *acquiesce* to being treated as second-class citizens. Jesus' instruction to *serve* rather than overthrow the Roman empire was the *last* thing they wanted to hear from the One who called himself their Savior.

And to be fair, we don't love it either. In the two thousand years since Jesus spoke these words, we've twisted, ignored, or interpreted them to mean anything *other* than what He plainly said. The pre-Jesus doctrine of "an eye for an eye" just *feels* better. We love getting back at people for the harm they've done to us, so much so that we once championed duels as the *most* honorable way of responding to a personal offense. As moralist Samuel Johnson said, "A man may shoot the man who invades his character, as he may shoot him who attempts to break into his house."[1] Such reasoning makes perfect sense to us, and yet "invasions of character" were precisely what Jesus instructed us to overlook.

## Political Correctness

Sadly, Mr. Johnson wasn't the only one who missed the mark in condoning duels as an appropriate means of addressing offense.

Today, Christians similarly condone such duels—though with words, rather than guns. We see this in the news, on social media, and in pulpits across America, where believers justify their offensive words by masquerading them as "truth." This is especially prevalent in politics when Christians on both sides of the aisle think that their beliefs align most closely with God's.

Take, for example, the issue of political correctness. As a staunch proponent of the First Amendment, it incenses me when the progressive Left uses political correctness to censor much-needed dialogue regarding the moral and social issues of our day. By wielding political correctness like a weapon, they offend some in the name of preventing further offense to others. Not only does this lower the quality of our political engagement, but it also distorts the use of political correctness as originally intended. Used properly, as a means of preventing further marginalization of certain people groups, political correctness is something I think Jesus would have actually championed as a higher standard of speech.

Nevertheless, Christians on both sides of the aisle misuse political correctness as a justification for offending. Those on the left use it to bludgeon and silence those on the right by labeling them racist, sexist, or any other "ist" that shuts them down. In attempting to force their worldview on others, they become fixated on their version of justice, and when others disagree, they threaten to cancel them. While their offensive words and actions often stem from their desire for justice, they minimize their effectiveness in the political arena. Worse, they compromise their witness for Jesus, and divide the church further, by labeling half good and the other half bad—something Jesus never would have done.

Meanwhile, Christians on the right reject political correctness as outright lies and counter them with "straight talk" devoid of love. Many selectively contrast biblical correctness against political correctness while ignoring the fact that Jesus spoke truth with both grace and honor. Their labeling of that which they deem to be politically correct subtly positions their beliefs as "the norm," rendering others' abnormal. Doing so makes them spiritually and intellectually lazy for dismissing perspectives they don't like as "politically correct nonsense" rather than consulting God on what to think about them.

By using political correctness offensively, both sides forget that Jesus' harshest words were reserved for those who were legally, religiously, and morally correct, but thoroughly unloving. Like the Pharisees, we can do everything right and still miss the point. And when we do, Jesus warns us that serious repercussions lie ahead.

## The Significance of Woe

In revisiting Luke 17:1, we see that Jesus issues a warning we might have otherwise overlooked: "Woe to the one through whom [offenses] come!" (CSB). Since we don't use the word *woe* in everyday English, I looked it up and learned that it means "deep suffering from misfortune, affliction, or grief"[2]—not a momentary regret, or a passing sense of remorse. Woe is far weightier a fate, and Jesus reserves its use for the most egregious people and behavior. This is evidenced by the tongue-lashing he gave the Pharisees in Matthew 23, when He declared "woe" on them not once or twice, but *seven* times—a sampling of which follows:

> Woe to you, teachers of the law and Pharisees, you hypocrites! You shut the door of the kingdom of heaven in people's faces. You yourselves do not enter, nor will you let those enter who are trying to. . . .
>
> Woe to you, teachers of the law and Pharisees, you hypocrites! You give a tenth of your spices—mint, dill and cumin. But you have neglected the more important matters of the law

—justice, mercy and faithfulness. You should have practiced the latter, without neglecting the former. You blind guides! You strain out a gnat but swallow a camel. . . .

Woe to you, teachers of the law and Pharisees, you hypocrites! You are like whitewashed tombs, which look beautiful on the outside but on the inside are full of the bones of the dead and everything unclean. In the same way, on the outside you appear to people as righteous but on the inside you are full of hypocrisy and wickedness.

vv. 13, 23–24, 27–28

Jesus concludes His laundry list of woe-inducing actions by calling the Pharisees "a brood of vipers" (v. 33) whose paths would eventually lead them to hell. Clearly, woe carries heavy spiritual, physical, and emotional repercussions. But who would have ever thought that normal, everyday offensiveness— something you and I barely consider "sinful," given how regularly it's championed in both politics and the church—would result in the same "ruinous trouble" the Pharisees were destined to suffer? And if being offensive makes us modern-day Pharisees, what choice do we have but to rid our lives, actions, and words of anything—other than the gospel itself—that causes offense?

## Trading Love for Offense

As always, questions like these have obvious "right" answers. But doing the right thing is much harder in a political environment that champions offense over love.

I ran for Congress in an election year characterized by offensive comments that were either whitewashed as truth or applauded as strength. Honoring my enemies caused many in my own party to label me—a woman who'd spent her entire life working to get conservatives elected—a RINO (Republican in Name Only). I'll never forget a debate in which that happened. I'd prepared for days and knew my facts and positions inside out and backwards. My primary opponent did not, but everything she said was combative, insulting, or offensive. The audience ate her act up, while my answers fell flat.

To my liberal-hating audience, it didn't matter that my positions were more conservative than my opponent's. All they wanted was a fighter who would throw partisan bombs and "sock it to the Left." I ended up losing that debate—not in substance, but in form. Choosing honor over insults and facts over rhetoric caused my audience to label me both "moderate" and "weak"—when I was actually neither and what they really meant was "she's just not mean enough."

The trade-off they wanted me to make simply wasn't worth it to me. Honoring God and my opponents mattered more than pleasing an audience that wanted blood. My decision to take the high road eventually paid off when all but the most partisan extremists in our party voted for me on election night. I won by a comfortable margin over the woman whose primary campaign tactic was being offensive.

But even if I'd lost, I still wouldn't have changed a thing. As a Christian, I'm held to God's standards, not the Republican party's. And since I'd launched my campaign on Jesus' principles of honor, love, and respect, I was committed to them. As the only Christian on the ballot, I knew that folks were watching how I responded to attacks on my family and character. They wanted to know if what I believed was real or just a campaign gimmick. And on a deeper level, I knew that what they were really looking for was proof of Jesus' love in me.

More than anything, I wanted them to find what they were looking for. If the only thing they got out of my campaign was that Jesus loved them, that would have sufficed for me. I love God more than my own political ambitions and care more about pleasing Him than man. The fact that God helped me suppress my all-too-human desire to offend is the best evidence of His power in my life. No matter how weak that made me look to some, loving God and others was worth it.

I'll readily admit, however, that it wasn't always easy, and I still struggle at times to obey Him. For the first few months of my campaign, all I wanted to do was fight. Behind closed doors, I talked a lot of trash and justified offensive things I said about my opponents as "blowing off steam" or "speaking among friends." But no matter how I characterized it, doing so made me just as guilty of being offensive as those who'd offended me. Recognizing the toll this took on both my witness and my spiritual well-being, I asked friends and supporters to pray for my heart toward my opponents. Doing so aligned my heart with God's, which made it easier to be less offensive and more loving. It's worth mentioning, too, that my struggles in this regard gave me a lot more grace for the ministry leader who disappointed me at the age of twenty-two.

I'm finally learning, after years of doing it wrong, that if we truly want to honor God, we must reject offensive words, labels, and tactics. Sure, they may help us win an election or two, but the spiritual damage they inflict far outweighs their benefits. No election is worth sacrificing our witness. As Jesus asked, "What does it profit a man to gain the whole world, and forfeit his soul?" (Mark 8:36 ESV). The answer is it doesn't. There's only one surefire way to win in life and politics: by rejecting offense and trading it for love. To that end, here are some ideas for ridding our hearts of offense once and for all.

**Let God define "offense."** Since we live in a culture of contempt, offending someone is inevitable if we have any opinion whatsoever. What matters, then, is what *God* thinks about our words—not what our ever-shifting culture says about them.

Speaking God's truth is a commandment, no matter how offensive it might be. There's no "out" for distinguishing right from wrong and being bold in declaring it so. Throughout

Scripture, the prophets, teachers, disciples, and even Jesus himself spoke biblical truths that were offensive to many. But because their intentions were pure, they spoke with God's blessing, authority, and anointing, and changed the culture around them.

God can use anyone and anything to convey His truth to the world. However, His anointing is lifted from those who speak His truth when the sin of pride creeps into their hearts. Pride adds to the offense of the gospel by making us offensive to the world around us. Rude, obnoxious, and self-righteous politicking both minimizes our influence and misrepresents God's heart for the world. As such, being offensive to others offends God as well, since He cares as much about how we treat those we disagree with as what we stand for.

Speaking the truth in love is the only way to safeguard us from offending God. Jesus understood this principle well, so when His disciples asked, "Did you know how upset the Pharisees were when they heard what you said?" (Matthew 15:12 MSG), Jesus shrugged them off and said, "Forget them" (Matthew 15:13–14 MSG). His heart was pure, and His words were loving, so He didn't have to worry about how His message landed. In all that He did and said, Jesus focused on the only thing that mattered: pleasing His Father by doing and saying what He asked of Him. Neither well-meaning friends nor ill-intentioned foes could deter Jesus from full obedience and submission. By appealing to an audience of One, Jesus increased in favor with God and man, and gave us a higher standard to aspire to.

**Engage your "enemies" on their turf.** Political debates turn into shouting matches when neither side feels like it's being heard. We're so used to ignoring, dismissing, and invalidating those we disagree with that we rarely take the time to try to understand their positions. We end up talking over each other rather than listening and working together, which is why so many people hate politics and avoid engaging altogether.

Jesus, however, modeled a different way of engaging with those who considered themselves His enemies. Take, for example, the woman at the well, whom Jesus literally went out of His way to meet. Most Jews would never journey through Samaria, given their disdain for the Samaritan people. But Jesus went straight to Samaria in order to express His love to a woman who'd been shunned by her own people. Jesus broke many Jewish customs by talking to a Samaritan, talking to a woman, and treating His "enemy" kindly. His purpose, however, wasn't merely to show her kindness, but to reveal His divine nature by asking her questions that were deeply meaningful and personal to her. As a result, she felt known, accepted, and loved by Jesus, which changed the trajectory of her life as well as the spiritual welfare of the town she lived in (John 4).

When we detour from our own agendas to meet people where they are, we emulate Jesus' formula for winning hearts and minds. President Bush modeled this beautifully when he prioritized pursuing the hearts and minds of Latino voters. Though clearly not Latino himself, he always went out of his way to meet with Hispanic leaders and asked them how he could help improve their lives. He did so because he wanted them to know that he valued and appreciated them—not only as constituents, but as fellow Americans and friends.

After President Bush was elected, I joined him for a meeting with the top thirty-five Latino leaders in America—thirty-four of whom were outspoken Democrats. Many of them confessed to secretly voting for him, and I had to ask them why. After all, their politics aligned more with our opponent's than ours, and on many issues we were diametrically opposed.

Their answers were uniform and telling: "We feel like President Bush likes and respects us because he always solicits our opinions on the issues that matter most to our communities. We don't always agree on solutions, but he never lets our disagreements come between us. He takes the time to listen and understand us, and that means more to us than any pandering politician's words." I learned a critical lesson that day: political alignment, while important, is less influential than making others feel seen, heard, and known. By meeting them on their turf, President Bush turned his political "enemies" into friends—and they rewarded him by voting for his reelection in record numbers four years later.

**Personify love.** Love is the culmination of every commandment God has ever given us. Doing anything, even "good" things, is futile when it isn't done in love. As Scripture says, we can speak "in tongues of men and angels," "have the gift of prophecy," "fathom all mysteries and knowledge," "have faith that moves mountains," and "give all we have to the poor," but if we do any of these separate from love, we get zero credit from God (1 Corinthians 13:1–3).

So how do we stay focused on loving others while engaging in strife-ridden politics? The Bible's prescription is clear: "Love is patient, love is kind. It does not envy, it does not boast, it is not proud. It does not dishonor others, it is not self-seeking, it is not easily angered, it keeps no record of wrongs. Love does not delight in evil but rejoices with the truth. It always protects, always trusts, always hopes, [and] always perseveres" (1 Corinthians 13:4–7). By following this formula, we *become* love—and by extension, inoffensive—even to those who hate everything we represent as truth.

In Jesus, we have an example of One who loved perfectly while being intensely persecuted for His beliefs. Jesus lived a life that was so far above reproach that the only faults His enemies could find were in His convictions. Unlike the felons who hung on either side of Him, Jesus was crucified for the truth He represented, rather than any untoward behavior. Thus, the guilt lay squarely on those who called for His crucifixion rather than on our sinless Savior himself.

Those of us who follow Jesus should strive to love perfectly, just like our Savior did. We'll fail of course, and miserably at that, but what matters to God is that we keep on trying. By striving to personify love, we'll naturally become less offensive and help keep the focus on God's agenda rather than our own shortcomings. And by getting out of God's way, we can better channel His anointing and power, which will help us catalyze change like never before.

## REFLECTION

1. What aspects of your political engagement are offensive to God and others?
2. How do you define *offense*—by the world's standards, or God's?
3. What can you do to change how you engage so that your political actions and words are inoffensive to God?

## PRAYER

*Lord, I confess that the things I say and do in the name of being right are often intended to get a rise out of others. And I recognize that the offense I cause both hurts your heart and ruins my witness. Help me to change my tone and the words I use so that I reflect your love for others. And if I do cause offense, let it be because of the Truth I speak rather than how I say it. In Jesus' name, Amen.*

# 7

# UNSHAKABLE

Of all the needs . . . the one that must be satisfied . . . is the unshaking need for an unshakable God.

—Maya Angelou

September 11, 2001, started off like any other workday. I couldn't find a matching shoe for the one I already had on, and my coffee was taking its sweet time brewing. I tapped my fingers on the countertop, willing the coffeemaker to respond by quickening its drip. Looking at my watch only made me more anxious: "8:17" it read, meaning I was seven minutes late. "Please God, let there be less traffic this morning," I prayed aloud as I searched for my missing shoe.

A few minutes later, I rushed to the car, travel mug in hand. As I yanked the door open, the top popped off the mug, and coffee spilled all over my cream-colored suit. "UGGGH!" I yelled at nobody in particular as I ran back into my house to change.

At 8:25 a.m., I jumped back into my car, sporting a slightly wrinkled navy suit. It was the same one I'd worn a few days earlier at the arrival ceremony for Mexican President Vicente Fox. It wasn't exactly fresh-smelling—after all, I'd worn it for hours on the South Lawn of the White House on a warm September day. But as a twenty-three-year-old making a paltry political salary, my options were limited. So I sprayed my suit with a bottle of Febreze and prayed that nobody at the office would notice.

On most mornings, I tuned into WTOP, Washington's local AM radio station for weather, news, and traffic. However, that morning I chose silence instead and spent my entire commute coming up with an apology to offer my boss for showing up late to work. Four miles and thirty minutes later, I pulled into the Ellipse, where all the junior White House staffers parked. Parking was never guaranteed, since there were more of us than there were spots, but thankfully, I found one—albeit the farthest one from the office.

As I jogged toward the West Executive Avenue entrance, I sensed a nervous tension in the air. White House employees usually treated each other more like teammates than colleagues, but this morning, everyone looked stressed, hurried, and upset. Even the Secret Service agents, who could always be counted on for a laugh, seemed tense, irritable, and distracted. I even saw a few SWAT team officers—the ones dressed in black who were usually hiding in the bushes—milling around in the open with guns. *Interesting,* I thought, but shrugged it off as I rehearsed my apology for the hundredth time.

Rather than wait for the "historic" (read: slow) elevator to fetch me, I ran up five flights of stairs in the Old Executive Office Building. I glanced at my watch—"9:04" it read, as I pushed the door to the office open. My heart pounded, as much from the cardio as the fear of being reprimanded. *Please, Lord, let them be merciful!* I prayed as I stepped into the office. But as soon as I saw the looks on my coworkers' faces, I realized that I was the last thing on their minds.

## The Day That Shook America

"What's happening?!" I asked everyone and nobody in particular.

"It's just awful," my boss answered, pointing at one of the many TVs in our office. I glanced at the one closest to me and witnessed a horror I will never forget: the World Trade Center's twin towers engulfed in flames and the dust-covered faces of those escaping them. A hijacked plane had hit the second tower moments before I entered the office, and everyone was in shock.

As I watched the towers burn, my colleagues filled me in on all the events I'd missed. I learned that the first tower had been hit twenty minutes earlier, while I was driving to work. As I pieced the morning together, everything started to make sense: the fact that I was able to get a parking spot that late in the morning, the abnormally light traffic driving into the district from Virginia, the overt presence of SWAT team members, and the eerie tension I felt in the air walking into work. While I'd spent the morning worrying about my job, everyone else had spent theirs fretting over our country.

Suddenly my telephone rang, startling everyone in our otherwise silent office. I ran over to my desk to grab it, whispering, "Hello?"

"Denise . . . it's Anne. Can you believe what's happening?"

Anne was a friend I'd worked with on the campaign who'd moved with me from Austin to work in the Bush administration. She'd taken a position at the Pentagon, working for our former colleague who was a high-ranking presidential appointee in the US Air Force.

"I can't, Anne. I literally have no words," I replied.

A lump swelled in my throat as we sat in silence, comforted by the fact that we were mourning together. Having worked on the campaign trail for over a year, we'd experienced numerous ups and downs. But all that we'd been through paled in comparison to what we were about to experience. This attack on our nation shook us to the core as we processed what it meant for our country, our military, and ourselves.

My heart ached as we exchanged a few more words, then promised to call each other later. Right as I hung up, our office door burst open, and a Secret Service officer yelled, "Get out of the building NOW!" I looked at my colleagues, who all seemed shell-shocked, and sprang into action. "Let's go, everyone!" I yelled as I grabbed my purse, an elderly volunteer, and a terrified intern. SWAT team members flooded the White House grounds, making it look like we'd been invaded by a swarm of ants. I walked as fast as I could in my heels until a Secret Service agent yelled, "Take off your shoes and run!" I looked at him as he looked at the sky, and panic set in. Clearly he knew something that I didn't, so I did as I was told and ran.

In the time that it took to run to my car, the Pentagon had also been hit. I switched my radio to the local news station and listened to eyewitness reports of the horror unfolding mere miles from me. My drive home took me right past the Pentagon, so I spent the next two hours in bumper-to-bumper traffic, staring at black smoke and flames. Thousands of Pentagon employees walked on the side of the highway, looking like extras in a post-apocalyptic zombie movie. As I watched them wander in a daze, I wondered if my friend Anne was okay. I knew that her boss's office was on the side that had taken a direct hit, but I had no way of checking in on her since all cell service in the DC region had been knocked out. I cried out to God, begging Him to protect her, and prayed for her family as well.

My paradigm of the world shifted that day. I was personally connected to hundreds of people who were directly affected by the attacks. White House colleagues aside, many of my college friends worked in or near New York's financial district. My friends at the Pentagon, including Anne (who I later learned was safe), had all lost friends and coworkers. Barbara Olson, a conservative commentator whom I admired enormously, was killed on Flight 77. And friends and family members who served in our military readied themselves for war.

## Fear and Politics

To say that 9/11 turned my world upside down is a vast understatement. For weeks, I cried daily, if not hourly. Unable to sleep, I watched cable news networks throughout the night, seeking every detail I could about the terrorists and our war against the Taliban. During the work week, my focus was aligned with the administration's, doing all we could to help America get back on track. And during the few hours a week that I wasn't working, I fretted over the possibility of yet another attack.

I grew up in a time of relative peace, and 9/11 shattered the sense of security I'd always taken for granted. Like a soldier suffering from PTSD, I lived in a constant state of hypervigilance. Every loud noise and low-flying plane set my nerves on edge, and everywhere I went, I looked for evidence of terrorism and foul play. Fear and paranoia consumed me, driving me to work harder and stay watchful.

My only consolation was learning that I wasn't alone in how I felt. I knew this because politicians like the ones I worked for have the world's best pollsters on their payrolls. The RNC, DNC, and every other political organization in Washington always have their fingers on the pulse of Americans. They knew exactly how we felt before, during, and after 9/11, and precisely how to use that information to their advantage.

In the wake of the terrorist attacks, pollsters found that 49% of Americans felt as though their sense of security had been fundamentally shaken.[1] Seventy-one percent said that they felt depressed, 63% said they couldn't stop watching the news, and a third reported having trouble sleeping.[2] A vast majority of Americans said they were very (28%) or somewhat (45%) worried about another attack.[3] And when asked a year later to describe how their lives had changed, about half said they felt more afraid, more distrustful, or more vulnerable as a result of the attacks.[4]

In short, our frazzled nerves and loss of control shattered our sense of security. And politicians, many of whom I believe felt a deep and sincere sense of responsibility to the American people, were also wise enough to know how to leverage our fear to their advantage.

The use of fear in politics is a time-tested strategy, as evidenced by leaders throughout history. Fear is one of the most polarizing forces in human nature and has always been exploited by the ruling class to sustain their power. John Adams admitted as much at the dawn of our nation, writing that "Fear is the foundation of most governments."[5] World history proves the truth of his statement: from the Peloponnesian War to Nazism, the rise of Stalin and Mao to the war on ISIS, fear has precipitated more global strife than any other single emotion. American history has proven the same, as evidenced by Jim Crow laws, Japanese internment, and the Chinese Exclusion Act, to name a few.

Rather than hide their use of fear as a political tactic, some politicos openly embrace it. A leading consultant asserted that rather than less fear, "we need more fear" in American politics.[6] He likened its use in campaigns to warning signs in dangerous situations, acknowledging its benefits but none of its downsides. He also said that the best consultants use fear implicitly, rather than explicitly, to avoid being accused of manipulating the public. "The only one who's ever accused of using fear tactics in a campaign is the guy who loses, and that's a rule."[7]

His defense of fear as a legitimate political strategy tells me a lot about what we're willing to accept as fair game in American politics. But sadder yet is the fact that so many Christians buy into it, despite God's admonitions to resist fear. We need to recognize that fear is the Enemy's tactic—not God's. As such, giving in to fear, or worse, perpetuating it ourselves, puts us on the wrong side of spiritual battle lines.

## Feeling v. Feeding Fear

At the end of the day, it's up to each of us to decide whether we're buying what this consultant is selling. To be clear, I'm not knocking fear as a legitimate feeling that all of us experience at times. *Feeling* fear is completely understandable when terrifying truths are brought to light. But *feeding* fear is a decision, whether conscious or not, that flies in the face of everything God tells us in Scripture. Moreover, it's one of the Enemy's most effective tactics for controlling our minds, emotions, and votes, the consequences of which are negative and significant.

**Fear is humanistic.** I can't tell you how many times I've heard the words, "I'm moving to Canada if so-and-so gets elected." As a daughter of a Canadian immigrant, I laugh every time I hear them uttered. Most Americans wouldn't survive a winter up north, even if they tried. My Canadian father admits that he moved from Ontario to California to avoid turning into a popsicle. Each and every winter, that's a decision I thank him for making on our family's behalf!

Joking aside, the message their words convey is that our welfare is dependent on election outcomes. That line of reasoning makes total sense for those who don't know God and are humanistic in their thinking. After all, if all we have is this short life on earth, and someone we disagree with has some measure of control over it, then it's logical to think that losing an election would seem like the end of the world.

But as Christians, we know this isn't true, since God is the only One who has any say over our destinies. As one of our most beloved Scriptures reads, "'I know the plans I have for you,' declares the Lord, 'plans to prosper you and not to harm you, plans to give you hope and a future'" (Jeremiah 29:11). These were promises given to the Israelites by God himself as they were exiled from Jerusalem to Babylon, where they had no political power or influence and lived at the mercy of a king who was an enemy of the Jewish people. Even so, God did as He promised and made the Israelites thrive in the midst of their enemies, proving that God's power over our lives is greater than any ruler's could ever be.

**Fear is contagious.** Researchers from the California Institute of Technology sent groups of friends through a haunted house to study the social effects of fear. They found that the more friends that participants had with them while touring the haunted house, the more frightened they felt walking through it. This phenomenon is known as "fear contagion": the notion that your body picks up on your friends' signals and experiences a heightened state of fear when others express theirs, even in the *absence* of any specific startles or spooks.[8] The mere fact that their friends felt afraid was all it took for them to feel the same way.

Now consider the impact that fear contagion has on our political atmosphere today. Check out the Nielsen media ratings, and you'll quickly see that the talking heads who scare us most also have the most viewers. Or look at FEC filings, which tell us which politicians raise the most money. It's almost always the "Chicken Little" crew, who tell us that the sky is perpetually falling. By stoking our fears, candidates make us receptive to their promises of protection. All they ask for in exchange is our money, our votes, and our peace.

As discerning Christians, we must stop buying into the fear narrative that is so prevalent in our politics. Any sense of security that a human being offers is completely and utterly false. As the saying goes, "Safety is not the absence of danger, but the presence of God." Our hope lies in God's protection alone, and our words and actions should reflect this truth.

**Fear makes us irrational.** Behavioral scientists tell us that two primary desires govern our actions: the desire to avoid pain or loss and the desire to seek pleasure or gain. Researchers have found that when presented with this binary choice, we choose loss avoidance more than twice as often as we do the pursuit of gain.[9] In other words, we're more motivated by the fear of losing something than we are by the potential for gain.

In politics, our fear of loss causes us to vote *against* what we're afraid of rather than *for* what we know is best. When we operate from a position of fear, strategic decision-making is cast to the wayside, and survival becomes our primary goal. Rather than look for ways to expand our authority and influence, we hunker down and crouch into a defensive mode. Such a posture projects defeat rather than victory and causes us to fight among ourselves for what God has already promised us all.

**Fear divides us.** Fear causes separation and isolation, which lead to distrust, misunderstanding, and hatred. This is why theologian Howard Thurman tells us that "fear is the great enemy of community."[10] No single human emotion is more divisive than fear.

Jesus prescribes a very different end game for His followers. As Christians, we are called to live in unity, by loving one another and being gracious regarding our differences in opinion. Love is thus the antidote to fear, as well as its evil twin, division. As Scripture says, "Perfect love casts out fear" (1 John 4:18 ESV). Fear and love cannot coexist.

But be prepared to swim against the current of culture if you decide to trade your fear for love. Many in politics—including Christians—will caution you against losing your grasp on reality. "Don't be naïve," they'll say, "or you'll be taken for a fool." Fear causes even well-meaning people to try to convince you of your naïveté when you choose to embrace rather than reject those you disagree with.

Jesus, however, welcomed His enemies rather than push them away. Even in the moment of His deepest betrayal, Jesus healed the high priest's servant's ear and called Judas His "friend" (Luke 22:51; Matthew 26:50). His example proves the power of love over fear, and that embracing our enemies is always the godly response.

## Fear v. Truth

My reality, like most believers', begins and ends with the Word of God. So here are the spiritual truths that I cling to when fear threatens to influence my thinking.

**God is for us.** In Romans 8:31, Paul says, "If God is for us, who can be against us?" I love this verse because it reminds me that mere mortals' power and authority are no match for God's. This is a fabulous starting point for a shift in our perspective since it reminds us to place our hope in God rather than in man. When we're on God's side, He's on ours, and nothing any human can do will prevent His plans from coming to pass.

**God has given us the power to overcome fear.** One of my favorite verses of Scripture reads, "God has not given us a spirit of fear, but of power and of love and of a sound mind" (2 Timothy 1:7 NKJV). I recite this verse any time I feel fearful, since it reminds me that I have a supernatural advantage over fear because I have the mind of Christ (1 Corinthians 2:16). However, that doesn't mean that I will never feel fear again—as humans, we all do. Rather, it reminds me to submit my thoughts to the Lord and declare His promises over everything I fear. When I do so consistently and with conviction, fear loses its control over my mind. Hope, rooted in God's character and promises, overcomes me instead.

**God promises us an abundant life.** In John 10:10, Jesus tells us that the Enemy comes to steal, kill, and destroy, but that He has come to give us life in abundance. Some take this promise to mean that we'll have material, physical, or political abundance in this world—that things will always go our way and life will be rosy. But anyone who's lived a little knows that life can be anything *but*, and that God's promises nevertheless remain true.

The fact is, Jesus can help us thrive no matter who's in charge, because God meets all of our needs himself (Philippians 4:19). This truth stands in stark contrast to promises made by our political parties, who point to the man-made institution of government as our be-all and end-all. Nothing could be further from the truth, as nothing of real significance can come from the hands of humans. God may use our leaders as a conduit of His provision, but He is our ultimate Source and the only One we need.

**God is sovereign.** Colossians 1:16–17 reads, "For by him all things were created, in heaven and on earth, visible and invisible, whether thrones or dominions or rulers or authorities—all things were created through him and for him. And he is before all things, and in him all things hold together" (ESV). This passage reminds us that God truly is sovereign, and that nothing happens or exists in this world that isn't subject to His authority.

Lest we think that politicians are an exception to this rule, Scripture emphasizes the fact that *God* is the one who appoints our leaders. In the book of Romans, one verse states this principle twice: "There is no authority except that which God has established. The authorities that exist have been established by God" (Romans 13:1). What's remarkable about this verse is that Paul wrote these words during the reign of Nero, who was one of the most notorious persecutors of Christians in the history of the church. Paul obviously knew of Nero's wickedness, but he instructed believers not to question Nero's legitimacy or God's decision to put him in power. Rather than incite a rebellion to overthrow Nero, Paul instructed the church to submit to God's plan by submitting themselves to His chosen leader. Paul knew that God was sovereign over the Roman government, however evil its leader was. And in the same way, we can trust in God's sovereignty and submit to the authorities, regardless of who He puts in charge of our country.

**God is faithful.** Second Timothy 2:13 reminds us that even when we're faithless, God "remains faithful—for he cannot deny himself" (ESV). Unlike our elected leaders, God doesn't flake on His promises. He stands by His Word and is enduringly faithful whether or not we hold up our end of the bargain. Therefore, we can trust His plans to come to pass, regardless of how faithful (or faithless) our leaders are.

One of my favorite hymns is "On Christ the Solid Rock I Stand." It's based on Matthew 7:24–27, which equates those who build their lives on the promises of God to those who build their houses on a firm foundation of stone. The hymn makes the point that rock-anchored structures are never in danger of being swept away. No matter how fierce the storms they face, they cannot be moved by anything other than the rock itself.

Similarly, it behooves us to anchor everything—including our hopes for good political leadership—to our ever-faithful God. When we do, no human, nation, or authority—no matter how rich, powerful, or influential they might be—can make us tremble in fear. By anchoring ourselves to God's faithfulness, we possess the peace that Jesus promises us. And when we do, His peace makes us completely and utterly unshakable.

## REFLECTION

1. How has fear affected your perspective of politics?
2. Are you feeding your fear or faith with what you believe about the people and parties who control our country?
3. What truths do you need to remind yourself of that will help you become unshakable?

## PRAYER

*Lord, I confess that I give in to fear when things spin out of control around me. Whether in politics or in my personal life, remind me of your power and authority over all things, people, and circumstances. Help me beat back anxiety by anchoring myself to who you are, and make me utterly unshakable, no matter who or what happens in our communities and nation. In Jesus' name, Amen.*

## 8

# TASTY AND BRIGHT

God's people are there to bring seasoning to an unsavory situation.

—Joyce Meyer

On November 7, 2016, I spent the evening bouncing between my campaign party and San Diego's Golden Hall, where candidates mingle with members of the media who camp out all night reporting on election returns. My staff had lined up a slew of interviews for me, and my last one just happened to be scheduled moments after the race was called for my opponent. "Jesus, help me," I prayed while tears of disappointment rolled down my cheeks.

Interviews are tough enough; doing one right after learning that you've lost a campaign takes more emotional fortitude, and mascara, than anyone should have to summon or wear. After pulling myself together, I was mic'd by the local station's media assistant. "I'm so sorry you lost," she said. "I was rooting for you!" Her sympathy made me feel both better and worse, prompting a new round of tears.

Fully mic'd and "hot," I took a deep breath, swallowed hard, and settled into my interview seat. *Whatever you do, DO NOT cry,* I instructed myself. I donned a "fake it till you make it" smile and prayed that God would use me somehow in spite of my emotions. *Please, Lord, help me get through this interview, and glorify yourself through it.*

I shook my interviewer's hand and waited for the countdown to go live.

3 . . . 2 . . . 1.

"Joining us now is Denise Gitsham, who ran as a candidate for the Fifty-second Congressional District. Denise, great to have you back with us, though I'm sure this is a difficult moment for you," the reporter opened. "A few minutes ago, your race was called for your opponent. I know he was favored in this race, but I can't imagine how disappointed you must feel." I nodded in agreement, fake smile intact, thinking *You have no idea.*

He continued, "Even so, you've got to feel proud of yourself, coming as close as you did—from a relative newcomer with no name identification to nearly 44% of the vote. Plus, you did it running a positive campaign, in an election season marked by mudslinging. How do you feel about the race you ran, and what would you like to say to those who supported you?"

"At my campaign kickoff a year ago, I pledged to run a different sort of race than what we've come to expect in politics, one marked by civility, honor, and respect for my opponents and constituents, both those I agreed with and those I did not." *Please, God, let the words I say next reflect these values.* "I didn't run a positive race because I'm a great person. I did it because that's the kind of candidate I figured God would be proud of. So while I'm saddened by the results of tonight's election, I want everyone watching to know that I respect your choice to reelect Congressman Scott Peters, and that I also respect his many years of public service to the people of San Diego.

"Of course, I'm incredibly grateful that the people in my district supported my race to the extent that they did. I will never, ever forget their generosity and kindness to me. The hours they spent knocking on doors, cold-calling voters, and working to pay for their contributions to my campaign will forever be etched on my heart and mind." *Okay, I made it. Now help me land this plane on solid, honoring ground.*

"As for Congressman Peters, I want him to know that as much as we disagree on the issues, I'm asking all my supporters to get behind him now that he's been reelected. I also want to offer my sincere congratulations. He ran a heck of a race and had a great team behind him. As long as San Diegans continue to reelect him, I'll be praying for his success. And if there's anything I can do to help him, I hope he'll call on me." *Whew.*

What happened next took me by surprise. My interviewer, a middle-aged man who came across as formal and unemotional, looked at me with misty eyes and a voice that broke ever so slightly as he said, "Denise, that's remarkable. I've never heard anyone say anything like that after losing a race. I really hope you run again. If we had more people like you in politics, I think we'd all feel a lot better about the state of our nation."

What my interviewer didn't know, and I did, was that the words I spoke weren't exactly mine. If it had been up to me, I would have skipped the interview entirely. Fortunately, God didn't let me miss an opportunity to reflect His love on a very public platform. I gave Him free rein to use me as His mouthpiece, and He followed through with His end of the bargain.

Throughout the interview, and over the course of my campaign, Jesus gave me many such opportunities to be salt and light in the political arena. But these opportunities aren't limited to politics; they exist for Christians in every sphere of influence. As believers, we are each commissioned to be cultural catalysts for Jesus—influencers, if you will. By *influencer*, I don't mean the type on social media who peddle fame and followers for money, but rather those who shift the atmosphere around them by being conduits of God's love. Being a God-influencer doesn't require an Instagram filter, or even a platform; all it takes is a willingness to show up, be authentic, and love whoever God puts in our path.

## The Significance of Salt

In Jesus' Sermon on the Mount, He tells His disciples that they are "the salt of the earth" (Matthew 5:13). This parable made perfect sense to people in Jesus' time, given how valuable salt was in their culture. For us modern-day disciples, however, it requires a little more explaining.

Unlike pepper, salt is in literally *everything*. As one of nature's most abundant materials, with more than 14,000 known uses, salt plays a central role in nearly everything we eat, touch, and wear. From paper to plastics, salt is a critical part of most industrial manufacturing processes. There's nothing more ordinary or common than salt, but its usefulness is nothing short of extraordinary.

Cooks have used salt since the beginning of time as an enhancer and preserver of food. God knew this when He created our taste buds and put salt into a flavor profile of its own. As Job asked in his namesake book, "Can that which is unsavory be eaten without salt?" (Job 6:6 KJV). The answer, of course, for this foodie is a resounding *no*.

In Jesus' day, salt also kept people from starving. Salt was rubbed into meat and fish to dehydrate proteins that would otherwise spoil, extending their shelf lives in times of scarcity. Its use as a preservative made salt so valuable that it became one of the first commodities ever to be traded. In some cultures, salt replaced currency, and in the Roman empire, soldiers were often paid with salt rather than money (their monthly *salarium* eventually became the English word *salary*). Salt didn't just flavor; it literally saved and sustained lives, making it even more valuable to Jesus' audience than it is to us today.

In Israel, salt was used to seal covenants between men and God. In 2 Chronicles 13:5, God gave eternal dominion over Israel to David and his sons through a permanent covenant of salt. The Israelites, similarly, used salt to seal their deals with each other. Particularly holy and inviolable obligations, such as marriage, were often designated "salt covenants."

Given all of salt's practical and spiritual applications, it makes perfect sense that Jesus would call His disciples the "salt of the earth." As with so many other good things in life, however, salt has a dark side when used "off-label" or in excess. Back in biblical times, salt was poured onto enemy land to destroy it, rendering it useless and barren. It was also used to punish Lot's wife, who disobeyed God and turned into a pillar of salt (Genesis 19:26). Today, we associate too much salt with health risks, such as hypertension and heart disease. Salt's dangerous side underscores the reality that salt can only be life-giving when used in the right context and quantity.

## Tasty v. Salty

God wants us to strike the perfect balance of salinity in our lives. In the context of politics, this could mean speaking truth, but doing so with honor toward those we disagree with; conducting ourselves with integrity while everyone around us lies or spins the truth; standing on the side of justice rather than siding with our own self-interest; or simply refusing to engage in trash-talking about people on the other side of the aisle. Politics offers countless opportunities for us to put our salt-shakers to use.

Despite our best intentions, however, we can sometimes find ourselves getting a little heavy-handed with the shaker, especially when we're passionate about what we're seeking to enhance. This is certainly true for me when I engage in politics. On many occasions, I've allowed what is objectively good—things like truth-telling, discernment, and honest disagreement—to turn into something that is objectively bad—things like shaming, judgment, and blaming others. Rather than using my salt to season a conversation, I open the cap and empty the shaker.

When this happens, I go from being tasty to turning salty. "Salty" people, in modern parlance, are miserable, bitter, and sarcastic individuals who make others feel hopeless about themselves and their circumstances. We're tasty when our words bring life to a situation, and salty when they bring death. Turning salty is thus the opposite of everything Jesus tells us to be.

For me, being salty comes more naturally than being tasty—especially when I'm emotional or upset. That's why my television interview was such a miracle; it could have gone either way, but God was gracious to make my words life-giving rather than destructive, petty, and bitter. I attribute this miracle, in part, to my own willingness to turn my shaker over to Him. The more faithful I am in surrendering it, the more likely He is to season me to perfection.

## Bold and Bright

In addition to being the salt of the world, Jesus also tells us that we're light. "You are the light of the world," He says. "A town built on a hill cannot be hidden. Neither do people light a lamp and put it under a bowl. Instead they put it on its stand, and it gives light to everyone in the house. In the same way, let your light shine before others" (Matthew 5:14–16).

As plain as this teaching seems on its face, it's worth pointing out a few of its nuances. In our "look at me" culture, it's tempting to think that being a light means drawing attention to ourselves. Social media influencers, for example, have made a living off of recording every detail of their lives. Our obsession with them has grown to the point that we look to them for guidance in how we shop, vote, travel, eat, work, and even worship. In many ways, we've become more obsessed with following *their* lights than we are with shining our own.

However, Jesus never intended the light He gave us to be used to impress others. Rather, He intended for us to reflect His light in order to help others find Him. None of us have inherent light that burns with any intensity. Rather, Jesus gave us His light—the light of Life, which we receive when we follow Him (John 8:12). Thus, Christians should not use the light He gives us for their own glory, but only for the Lord's.

God gives us His light to shine because it gives hope to the world. Like a light at the end of a tunnel, God's light keeps us moving forward when we'd rather throw in the towel. That's why God urges us not to hide it, but to put it on a lampstand for all to see (Matthew 5:15). His light is meant to be used and shared, just like our faith in Christ.

Reflecting God's light is critical for believers involved in politics. Americans desperately need hope, not in a politician or platform, but in the eternal hope of Christ. By shining His light as bright as we can, we illuminate their paths to Him. And once they find Him, their lights join ours to bring justice, love, and truth to the world.

## The Essence of Light

We all know that physical light helps us see, grow, and thrive. Light was one of God's original creations and the topic of His first recorded words in Scripture. "Let there be light!" the Lord pronounced in the third verse of the Bible (Genesis 1:3). God made light a prerequisite for life and contrasts it with the darkness that preceded it.

But as incredible as light is, it serves a much greater purpose than mere physical illumination. In the context of Scripture, light represents God himself. First John tells us that "God is light" (1:5). In the Gospel of John, Jesus affirms His deity by saying, "I am the light of the world" (8:12). King David writes in the psalms that "the Lord is my light and my salvation" (27:1), while the book of Revelation prophesies that "God will be their light" (22:5 ESV). Throughout Scripture, in both the New and Old Testaments, God and light are synonymous.

As God's children, we have the privilege of carrying His light within us. Jesus said, "Whoever follows me will not walk in darkness, but will have the light of life" (John 8:12 ESV). A few chapters later, Jesus imparts His light to us, calling us "children of light" (12:36). Paul affirms our identities as "children of the light" in his first letter to the church in Thessalonica (1 Thessalonians 5:5). And Paul reminds us that while we were "once darkness," we are now "light in the Lord," in the book of Ephesians (5:8).

The key to optimizing God's light in our lives lies entirely within our control. In order to benefit from the power of light, we have to turn it on. When we do, light beats back darkness, which cannot overcome it (John 1:5). We see this happen in the natural world whenever we flip a light switch on. Light doesn't struggle to overcome the darkness; it always easily prevails. As Martin Luther King Jr. so aptly remarked, "Darkness cannot drive out darkness: only light can do that."[1]

The "struggle" between light and dark, both metaphorically and literally, boils down to the choices we make. God can only encourage us to turn on His light; He can't make us do it. And while the benefits of living as light-bearers far outweigh the alternative, we often revert to living in darkness when we've chosen the world's way of doing things over God's.

Politically speaking, the benefits of light have never been clearer. God's light gives us the wisdom to discern His very best for our nation. That wisdom helps us make better decisions about who we elect as leaders, and which policies to support. It illuminates the dark underbelly of politics by revealing pride, deceit, and selfish ambition. And it empowers us to know precisely when and how to speak, engage, and act.

## Becoming Light-Bearers

God's light is what makes our civic engagement most effective and transformative. How, then, do we become bearers of His light in the political realm?

**First and foremost, by immersing ourselves in His Word.** In order to take a stand for truth, we've got to actually know what truth is. Knowing Scripture calibrates our minds to the truth, so that even when a political issue isn't explicitly addressed in the Bible, we can still make a well-educated guess as to what God thinks about it. As they say, "Knowing is half the battle!" and the Holy Spirit more than makes up for the other half.

**Second, by focusing on His light.** Scripture says that the eye is the lamp of the body, and that when our eyes are healthy, our bodies are full of His light. The opposite, however, is also true: when our eyes are unhealthy, our bodies are filled with darkness (Luke 11:34).

The point of this verse isn't how well we see, but rather what we focus on. When God is our focal point, hope floods our hearts and minds. That which seemed impossible suddenly seems redeemable. Instead of focusing on our own shortcomings, God's light focuses us on His power. Thus, we can be filled with hope even amid despairing circumstances.

But if we choose to focus on other things—such as our own strength, the failures of our leaders, or devastating news headlines—our bodies are guaranteed to be flooded with negativity and lies. Choosing what we focus on thus shapes our thoughts, emotions, and beliefs. By keeping our focus on God's light, we receive "the mind of Christ" (1 Corinthians 2:16) and are able to see things not only as they are, but as what God meant for them to be.

**Third, by believing in the power of His light.** Jesus tells us in the book of John to "believe in the light" (12:36). God's ability to effect change through us rests on the strength of our faith. In our minds, we know that with faith as small as a mustard seed, we can move mountains (Matthew 17:20). But knowing that doesn't change how we feel when the cards seem stacked against us.

This happens a lot in politics when "our side" is losing or things aren't going "our way." I admittedly slip into despair whenever things seem to be going awry, quickly forgetting that God's light in me is capable of making darkness retreat. In times like these, I channel the cry, "I believe; help my unbelief!" (Mark 9:24 ESV). Jesus always responds by bolstering my faith and resolve. When He refocuses me on *His* light, my perspective invariably shifts to hope.

**Fourth, by choosing to turn on God's light.** As noted above, we all must choose whether we turn God's light on in our own lives. In politics, that means we either choose to engage like Jesus or default to business as usual. There is no neutral ground between the two. Turning His light off leaves us and the nation in darkness and despair, while turning His light on leads us toward hope and redemption.

## Salt and Light Personified

Working in politics has taught me as much about what salt and light *isn't* as what it actually *is*:

It isn't judgmental,
It isn't harsh,

It isn't threatening,

It isn't prideful,

It isn't mean,

It isn't dishonoring, and

It doesn't make people want to run toward the exit when you walk into a room.

It *is* inspirational,

It *is* truthful,

It *is* honoring,

It *is* respectful,

It *does* unite,

It *does* inspire love, and

It *does* attract people like moths to a flame.

Someone once asked Nobel Prize winner Archbishop Desmond Tutu what role religious people should play in politics. His response was "They should be very active if they believe that the world belongs to God. . . . [But] if they don't act . . . as . . . the salt or the light, then things can go horribly, badly wrong."[2] In this statement, the archbishop accurately summarized the need for Christians to be the salt and light of the world. We should all take his advice to heart and strive to be as tasty and bright as God created us to be.

## REFLECTION

1. Are you more salty or tasty in the way that you engage in politics?

2. What aspects of politics do you think are in the greatest need of God's light and hope today?

3. How can you shine brighter for Jesus in the political realm?

## PRAYER

*Lord, you know my desire to be salt and light in everything that I do. But you also know that politics brings out the absolute worst in me! I'm heavier handed with my saltshaker and shine a little dimmer than I should, especially when I'm worried or upset about what's happening in politics. So season me, Lord, to perfection in every situation I find myself in. And help me keep your light switched on, so that I always reflect your grace, hope, and truth. In Jesus' name, Amen.*

# 9

# WISE AS SERPENTS

Do not heed the jar of man's warring opinions. Let God be
true and every man a liar.

—Horatius Bonar

As a child, I embraced everything my parents deemed patriotic.
Lee Greenwood's single "Proud to Be an American" was our
household soundtrack for years. An American flag flew on our
front porch, every dawn to dusk. Fourth of July was a family
affair where all three Gitshams marched in a red, white, and
blue parade. And when it came to politics, our litmus test was
simple: if you loved America, you were our candidate.

Politics were so black-and-white to me back then. Growing
up in a middle-class military town, everyone seemed to agree
with our perspectives. The only person who didn't was my
third-grade classmate Adam. We got into a heated argument
one fall day in 1984 when he casually mentioned that he supported Mondale. I laughed and rolled my eyes, telling him he

was stupid. Reagan was our man, and everyone I knew was voting for him, so Adam was clearly out of touch with reality.

Imagine my surprise when I left home for Maine to attend a college filled with people who agreed with Adam! Being at Bowdoin opened my mind to a whole new world of political ideologies. I was a government major and an American history minor, and my professors challenged me to rethink how I defined the term *patriotic*. While I only agreed with half of their suggestions, I learned to appreciate their perspectives. More importantly, they broadened mine enough to argue any side of an issue.

After graduating from college, I immersed myself in Republican politics, where my appreciation for opposing perspectives was no longer appreciated. Uniformity was the name of our campaign game, and everyone I worked with was a special brand of Texas conservative. Their "compassionate conservative" ideology turned classic conservatism on its head and was fueled by a heartfelt desire on Governor George W. Bush's part to bring out the very best in his constituents. *How* some campaigned to bring this ideology into fruition, however, was an altogether different matter.

At a weekly staff meeting, I raised my hand to ask whether a policy being considered was in the best interest of our constituents. The issue was a serious one for evangelical Christians and one that we'd made promises to them about. Another staffer laughed at me and said, "Who cares what they think?! Who else are they gonna vote for?" Fortunately, this particular staffer was an outlier in our campaign, which otherwise consisted of faith-filled people of integrity. But it did occur to me then and there that my fellow believers really had no recourse if we'd gone with the policy as proposed. Like my colleague said, they had no other choice in this election but to support Governor Bush. He was the only candidate who was pro-life and identified strongly with their faith. Fortunately for them, the rest of our senior staff was committed to upholding the Governor's (and their own) integrity. But I learned an important lesson that day: promises made can be easily broken when political expediency is at stake.

Years later, I sat at a fundraising dinner for a prominent politician. We were in a private dining room, and everyone else appeared to know each other. As the wine and Scotch flowed freely, so did the conversation. One donor was having a side conversation with those seated next to him, and when it came time for him to address the group, he pounded on the table and yelled, demanding to know when the campaign was going to drop "the anti-abortion crazies." He went on a minutes-long tirade against the influence of Christians on the Republican party. Everyone at the table nodded enthusiastically—at times "amen"ing his comments—including one individual who later rose to prominence courting Christians on behalf of the politician they were all there to support. When the donor's monologue ended, the campaign's representative said, "I hear you, and our candidate agrees with everything you're saying. But he needs their support in order to win, and he has to play along until he doesn't. We're keeping up the charade until after the election." The comments, so brazenly stated, were 180 degrees opposite of everything the politician had publicly promised. And in that moment, I felt sick to my stomach, knowing that Christians were being played.

Sadly, that wasn't the first or last time that I listened in on such conversations. Words like these, uttered behind closed doors, are more than often the norm. It's a well-known fact that politicos will say absolutely anything it takes to win. And when they do, their focus shifts to *staying* in power rather than following through on campaign promises.

These days, I rarely fall for strident platforms, empty promises, or lofty speeches made in the heat of the campaign. A candidate's words are mere starting points for me, helping me weed out who is and isn't in the running for my vote. Before I pledge my full support, I take Ronald Reagan's advice to heart: "Trust but verify."[1] I know way too much after 20-plus years in the game to be duped into selling my political soul.

My process for vetting a candidate requires patience and due diligence. I pay attention to their words, observe their behavior, and study the company they keep. I also research their past actions and public statements to see who they were when nobody was paying attention. Invariably, I find myself enamored with some, willing myself to believe better things about them than they deserve. And sometimes, I catch myself doing the very opposite simply because a candidate rubs me the wrong way. Whether positive or negative, I take all the information I've gathered and submit it to the Holy Spirit. By asking Him to make me wise as a serpent, I'm better able to discern who a candidate truly is (Matthew 10:16).

## God's Wisdom v. Ours

I once thought that being politically astute, or "in the know," equated to being wise. Knowledge, however, doesn't equate to wisdom, since we all have access to more information than ever, but few of us seem any wiser for it. *Without* the Holy Spirit's help interpreting what we see, read, and hear, all we have is information-fueled bias. *With* the Holy Spirit's help, however, we can see things from God's perspective.

In the book of Proverbs, King Solomon distinguishes between knowledge-based worldly wisdom and Spirit-filled godly wisdom. "Trust in the Lord with all your heart," he writes, "and lean not on your own understanding." (3:5). A few verses later, he warns us not to be wise "in our own eyes," but to "fear the Lord and shun evil" (3:7). In the New Testament, Paul writes, "If anyone among you thinks that he is wise, . . . let him become a fool [discarding his worldly pretensions and acknowledging his lack of wisdom], so that he may become [truly] wise. For the wisdom of this world is foolishness (absurdity, stupidity) before God" (1 Corinthians 3:18–19 AMP).

As these verses make crystal clear, worldly wisdom may impress other people and ourselves, but it never impresses God. Moreover, relying on our own wisdom often leads us astray. Our political situation grows dire when we seek the world's perspectives rather than God's. And more of the same cannot get us out of this bind; only a total reliance on God can.

## Get Wisdom

How, then, do we get godly wisdom? In the book of Proverbs, King Solomon says, "The beginning of wisdom is this: get wisdom" (Proverbs 4:7). His words imply that wisdom doesn't simply fall into our laps and that we must do something in order to get it. As he says in Proverbs 2:

> My son, if you accept my words and store up my commands within you, turning your ear to wisdom and applying your heart to understanding—Indeed, if you call out for insight and cry aloud for understanding, and if you look for it as for silver and search for it as for hidden treasure, then you will understand the fear of the Lord and find the knowledge of God.
>
> vv. 1–5

"Getting wisdom" is a lifelong, proactive process that requires:

- ☑ Accepting the Word of God as true
- ☑ Storing His commands in our hearts
- ☑ Turning our ears toward wisdom
- ☑ Applying our hearts to what we hear
- ☑ Calling out for insight

☑ Crying aloud for understanding

☑ Looking for wisdom as for silver

☑ Searching for wisdom as for hidden treasure

Given the list above, wisdom-seeking appears to be a full-time job—and truthfully, it is. However, choosing the world's ways leads us down a rabbit trail that is far more arduous and time-consuming to climb out of. That's why King Solomon urges us to get wisdom, "though it cost you all you have," for "wisdom is more valuable than rubies, and all the things that one desires cannot compare to her" (Proverbs 4:7; 8:11).

## The Importance of Asking

While there isn't a shortcut to getting wisdom, neither is there a magic formula. Jesus' brother James tells us that "if any of you lacks wisdom, let him ask God, who gives generously to all without reproach" (James 1:5 ESV). If we do, James promises that God will give us wisdom in spades. But when we ask, we must "believe and not doubt, because the one who doubts is like a wave of the sea, blown and tossed by the wind." (James 1:6–7). Both asking and believing are thus required of us in order to receive God's wisdom.

James's words are a helpful reminder to me because I often forget to ask God for wisdom. I either think I've got all the wisdom I need, or I go on autopilot and do things the way I always have. When things seem easy or familiar, I forget that our Mighty Counselor is still on standby. He never forces His wisdom on me if I don't ask for it. But when I do, Scripture's promise that "the Lord will give you understanding in everything" (2 Timothy 2:7 ESV) is fulfilled.

Admittedly, there are times when I'd rather *not* ask for His input, because I've already made up my mind. A decade ago, I fancied myself a political expert simply because I played one on a cable news network. The more I internalized my own chyron, the less I asked God for wisdom. Being enamored with my own knowledge made me value His wisdom less. This, in turn, made me deceive myself, and at the height of my own arrogance, I was dropped from the show. As Scripture warned fools like me, "Pride goes before destruction, and a haughty spirit before a fall" (Proverbs 16:18). I learned a hard lesson through that experience, which brought me back to asking.

## Chain of Fools

When I read the Bible, I'm comforted in knowing that I'm not the only fool out there. Take, for example, the Israelites, who with God's help removed everyone who stood in the way of their Promised Land. Eventually they got so good at winning that they stopped asking God for His help. Their victories made them think that *they* were special, so they relied on their own experience and wisdom rather than on God's.

It was then that a group of Gibeonites set out to deceive them. They knew that God had forbidden Israel from making treaties with resident nations like theirs. The Gibeonites didn't want to be forced out of their home, so they concocted a clever scheme with props and stories galore. When the Israelites showed up, they presented themselves as ragged and weary foreigners, saying, "We have come from a distant country [to ask you to] make a covenant with us" (Joshua 9:6 ESV).

Initially the Israelites were suspicious of their story, but eventually the Gibeonites talked them into agreeing to a covenant. Doing so put the Israelites in direct violation of God's orders, and when they discovered that they had been fooled, they were furious with the Gibeonites for deceiving them. The Bible, however, tells us that the Israelites only had themselves to blame. In dealing with the Gibeonites, they'd leaned on their own "wisdom" and "did not ask counsel from the Lord" (Joshua 9:14 ESV). As such, they were victims of their own arrogance, which kept them from accessing God's wisdom.

That wasn't the first or last time the Israelites paid dearly for rejecting God's counsel. Before God allowed them to enter the Promised Land, He led His people to walk in circles for forty years in the desert. God didn't do that because the Israelites were out of shape and needed to get their steps in. Rather, He did so because "they did not wait for his counsel" (Psalm 106:13 ESV) and chose their own paths instead.

## Birds of a Feather

It has been said that we are the average of the five people we spend the most time with.[2] So while seeking wisdom is an individual decision, living a lifestyle of wisdom requires good company. As Proverbs 13:20 says, "Whoever walks with the wise becomes wise, but the companion of fools will suffer harm" (ESV). Who we do life with has enormous influence over how wise we become.

For most of my life, I have purposefully associated myself with the wisest people I know. Some have impressive titles, while others do not, but the one thing they all have in common is that they're wise in the Lord. Growing up in Fairfield, California, I didn't always have access to the marketplace, ministry, and political leaders I now call friends. But I did have access to the godly and upstanding people who shaped my heart and mind in my formative years. Choosing wise friends has paid enormous dividends in every aspect of my life. The more time I spend with people like them, the wiser I become.

## Wisdom's Benefits

Culture tells us that ignorance is bliss, but Scripture says that wisdom's benefits are far greater.

> Blessed is the one who finds wisdom, and the one who gets understanding, for the gain from her is better than gain from silver and her profit better than gold. She is more precious than jewels, and nothing you desire can compare with her. Long life is in her right hand; in her left hand are riches and honor. Her ways are ways of pleasantness, and all her paths are peace. She is a tree of life to those who lay hold of her; those who hold her fast are called blessed.
>
> Proverbs 3:13–18 ESV

Since a long and pleasant life, riches, honor, peace, and blessings are things that I desire, growing in godly wisdom remains the top priority in my life.

Another important benefit of wisdom is that it protects us from untold evil. When Jesus sent His twelve disciples into the world, He warned them that they would be "like sheep among wolves." In order to protect their bodies, as well as their souls, He urged them to "be wise as snakes and innocent as doves" (Matthew 10:16). What Jesus meant by telling them this was that they needed God's wisdom to outsmart their enemies. But they also needed to remain pure in heart to succeed in their mission. Wisdom keeps our hearts pure while protecting us from evil (Ecclesiastes 7:12). And nowhere are enemies more ready to pounce than in the realm of politics.

## Applying Wisdom to Politics

In politics, we need godly wisdom now more than ever. As noted above, the best way to get it is to ask God for wisdom. It amazes me that we ask for God's help with everything else in our lives, from businesses to schools to families. But we rarely ask for God's help in choosing those whose policies influence and regulate them.

Perhaps one reason we fail to do so is that asking requires humility—a quality that's in short supply, especially in politics. When people think they have all the answers, they rarely seek confirmation from God. All they want is His stamp of approval, leaving very little room for Him to interject.

This was my dilemma when I opted out of voting for the first and only time in my life. I couldn't accept either candidate on the ballot for an office that would influence every issue I cared about. As I played the movie forward in my politicized mind, I concluded that both candidates were unworthy of my vote. Instead of asking for God's input on the matter, I decided not to vote at all. My pride prevented me from asking Him if there was something I was missing; instead of seeking the Lord's counsel, all I cared about was reserving the right to say, "I told you so."

Looking back at that election cycle, my political "smarts" prevented me from exercising wisdom. At the root of my resistance was my own ugly pride and selfish political ambition. I was too worried about what other people thought of me and how they'd react to anything other than the course of action I took. So I chose my gut over God's wisdom, which contributed to a suboptimal candidate winning.

Now that I've developed the habit of asking God for wisdom in navigating politics, I've also recognized how much I benefit from His discernment and protection. His wisdom exposes the lies of the Enemy, no matter how cleverly disguised they are. Whatever a party or candidate says, I ask God to reveal the truth behind it. As Scripture says, wisdom delivers us from evil (Proverbs 2:11–13), and nowhere does evil have greater potential to destroy our lives than through corrupt and wicked leaders.

Yet many of us rarely put to use what God offers us so freely. Instead of praying for wisdom about the right leaders and causes to support, we do the bare minimum—sometimes not even bothering to vote!—and wonder how we end up where we do. I'd be willing to bet that we spend more time picking produce at the grocery store than we do picking candidates in any given election.

When I shop for watermelons, for example, I pay very little attention to how "sweet and juicy" sellers claim they are. I literally go through a whole barrel of melons, knocking, smelling, and checking for bee stings to determine which ones are the best. When I come home, I'm almost guaranteed a good one and relish the fruits of my labor.

When it comes to picking candidates, however, most Americans are far more cavalier. We often vote for politicians based on the image they present rather than digging deeper to discern who they truly are. There is no sorting through, sniffing, or taking of closer looks—if they say what we like to hear, then we're satisfied in our choice. This explains why we're so disappointed in them after an election has been decided. A few months into watching them on the job, and we realize they've sold us a bag of goods. But what else should we expect, given how little effort we put into picking them? We can all afford to go home with a disappointing watermelon or two, but the ramifications of picking the wrong politicians can be disastrous.

There are plenty of practical steps we can take to do our own due diligence prior to an election. I always research what candidates have said and done *prior* to announcing their candidacy to get a sense of who they were before they stepped into the spotlight. I also research the companies, people, and organizations they're associated with to better understand where they invest their time, talents, and treasure. Voting in primaries is critical to making sure we have the best candidates to choose from when the general election rolls around. And attending town halls and candidate forums helps me get a feel for a candidate's moral compass and character.

Still, it's godly wisdom that ultimately helps us make the very best decisions. His wisdom equips us to see through those who seek to twist the truth and helps us elect leaders who reflect His love and will for us.

## REFLECTION

1. What aspects of your political engagement are lacking in godly wisdom?
2. Are your beliefs more influenced by your own biases or by wisdom from the Lord?
3. How can you be more intentional about seeking God's wisdom in politics?

## PRAYER

*Lord, I'm a fool for clinging to my own political beliefs instead of your wisdom and discernment. Help me distinguish between good and evil and show me when I'm being deceived. Make me innocent as a dove, and wise as a serpent, so that my political activities bear good fruit for our nation and your glory. In Jesus' name, Amen.*

# JUDGE PROPERLY

Judge with right judgment.
—John 7:24 ESV

Bob Marley was known for expressing gospel truths long before he became a reggae sensation. He was raised in the Pentecostal church, and his biblical knowledge made him an early standout in Sunday school. His Jamaican mother said that by the age of five, he had "a preachar's fire in him eye" that made her "lickle 'fraid sometime."[1]

It's no surprise, then, that his first recorded single was inspired by Scripture (Matthew 7:1) and titled "Judge Not." While a reggae beat makes this seem like a feel-good song, its lyrics urging us to "judge not before you judge yourself,"[2] make me feel more than a little uncomfortable. That's because I'm more than a little guilty of being a Judgy Judy myself.

As social beings, our understanding of others is critical to our survival. In order to make sense of their purpose and place in our lives, we tend to form snap judgments of others—in a tenth of a second, to be exact.[3] Researchers have found that first impressions form in children as young as the age of three, suggesting that judgment "appears in adultlike forms early in childhood and does not require prolonged social experience."[4] Moreover, first impressions persist due to a "primacy effect," influencing how we view people long after they've proven our impressions of them wrong.[5]

Given this reality, it's hard to imagine *anyone* being capable of doing what Marley (and Jesus) implores us to do. After all, God himself hard-wired us to be discerning about who we come in contact with. The Bible tells us that "man looks on the outward appearance" (1 Samuel 16:7 ESV). As such, *not* judging seems as impossible as not eating, sleeping, or breathing.

## Cutting Carbs

There are no two judgier groups of people alive than political and religious folks. Jesus hated the hypocrisy and pride that both groups represented because they elevated their own wisdom over God's. This caused them to think more highly of themselves than they ought, and made them judge others, including Jesus, as "less worthy."

In Mark 8:15, Jesus told His disciples to "beware of the leaven of the Pharisees and the leaven of Herod" (ESV). As usual, the disciples were very confused and chatted amongst themselves about bread. Jesus grew irritated at their ignorance, though to be fair, this was a cryptic teaching. As such, it requires some explaining, as well as a lesson in applicability.

The Pharisees were religious people who constantly challenged Jesus' deity. They clung to their works-based doctrines and demanded that Jesus perform miracles to meet their human standards (Mark 8:11). No matter how well Jesus answered their questions, or how many miracles He performed, nothing He did or said could ever satisfy them.

Herod represented the politicians of Jesus' day, who also rejected Him as Lord. Herod first appeared in Mark 6 in a story recounting the death of John the Baptist. In that account, when Herod Antipas heard about Jesus, he thought that Jesus was John the Baptist who had "come back from the dead" (Mark 6:16). Herod was impressed by Jesus' power but would not accept Him as Lord.

Jesus was nice to most people He met, but He wasn't particularly gentle with the Pharisees. He called their holier-than-thou attitudes "hypocrisy" (Luke 12:1) and described them using words that are nearly unfit to print (Matthew 23:13–37). Jesus also warned His followers to beware of the Herodians (Mark 8:15), a political party who opposed the Pharisees and sought to restore Herod to the throne in Judea.[6] One represented the religious spirit, the other the political spirit, both of which ran counter to the gospel by emphasizing human over spiritual deliverance. The teachings of both groups inspired a fear of man rather than a fear of God by championing humanity's discipline, strength, and works over Jesus' saving grace. Their self-professed "worthiness" made Jesus' grace an affront, causing them to treat Him as their enemy.

We have similar problems today, both in the church and in politics. In the church, Pharisaical leaven manifests as legalism; in politics, Herodian leaven manifests as extreme partisanship. While church is the right place to learn about the importance of good works, and politicians should always advocate for good policies and governance, we all need to be cognizant of how much of an emphasis we put on both compared to how focused we are on God's saving grace. If our goal is to be "good," "powerful," and "right" apart from God, we veer dangerously into worshiping humans and institutions—in the form of denominational dogma, pastors, political parties, and governmental leaders. Since no one can serve two masters (Matthew 6:24), we risk replacing the worship of Jesus with worship of human beings and institutions.

Judgment thrives when we think our survival depends on winning an argument or "being really good." Jesus attacked both lies head on, championing grace, mercy, and humility instead. Thus, the One who came "not to judge the world, but to save it" (John 12:47) fundamentally threatened the institutions of church and state. Both were so thoroughly infiltrated by the wrong leaven that they made Jesus out to be public enemy number one. That's why Jesus warned His followers to "cut the carbs." He didn't want them buying into heresy or misplacing their faith.

## Good Judgment

Throughout my faith journey and my political career, I've vacillated between being "righteously judgmental" and withholding judgment entirely. At times, I wasn't sure which to stick with, since some Scriptures made judgment sound like a good thing, while others made it seem bad. In the book of John, for example, Jesus says, "For judgment I have come into this world" (9:39). A few chapters later, however, Jesus says that He's come "not to judge, but to save" (12:47). Reading both statements a few chapters apart thoroughly confused me. So I dug deeper to find out what type of judgment, if any, Jesus actually condones.

As with all of Scripture, contextualization and reading multiple translations helps. In the context of His mission on earth, Jesus uses John 9:39 to assert His right to judge—in essence, by reiterating his deity. In the context of this chapter, Jesus uses a blind man whose sight He restores to lecture the Pharisees on the difference between physical and spiritual blindness. In *The Message* paraphrase, this verse reads: "I came into the world to bring everything into the clear light of day . . . so that those who have never seen will see." In other words, Jesus is saying His judgment is good because it opens the eyes of the spiritually blind to life-saving truth. Based on these verses and the context in which they're used, good judgment can therefore be characterized as: (a) rooted in truth, (b) spiritually illuminating, and (c) life-saving.

But if the notion of "good judgment" still sounds like an oxymoron—don't worry, you're not alone. We've moved so far from judging *anything* these days that we can hardly label things right or wrong without suffering serious repercussions. Like the leaderless Israelites who strayed far from God, we live in a culture where everyone does "what [is] right in [their] own eyes" (Judges 21:25 ESV). Good judgment is banned, or labeled as "hate," even when it's factually true and helpful. The fear of being labeled a "hating judger" has even removed judgment where it's needed most: in the church, where it technically belongs.

Further complicating things is the fact that our "no judgment" culture actually perpetuates *more* judgment. Since all of us are inherently judgmental by nature, judging those who judge others makes us all the likelier to judge each other. This reality underlies our cancel culture, which thrives on both sides of the aisle. With everyone feeling justified in choosing what they have a "right" to judge, everyone ends up right back where they started: being the Judgy Judy that nobody listens to or likes.

To offer us an exit from the judgment carousel, Jesus instructs us to "not judge according to appearance," but to "judge with righteous judgment" (John 7:24 NKJV). Judging by appearances positions us as God and comes most naturally to our flesh. But judging with righteous judgment keeps God as God and submits our standards to His.

Good judgment builds us up and directs us to God's truths. It fills us with holy conviction that makes us more committed to doing good. It exhorts us to be more Christlike and helps us to discern right from wrong. And it keeps us on the path of holiness, which helps us live in harmony with others.

Scripture is filled with examples of who and how God wants us to judge. Good judgment requires us to conform to these standards rather than abide by our own. When we do, we're anchored to God's truth, which helps us stay the course. Good and godly judgment keeps us from being swayed by ever-changing cultural standards of right and wrong.

## Bad Judgment

Bad judgment, on the other hand, is as destructive as good judgment is life-giving. Bad judgment seeks to shame rather than correct and is rooted in pride, anger, and hatred. It thrives on half-truths, exaggerations, and lies, so it offends, isolates, and divides us. Bad judgment not only hurts those we judge—it also exposes the sin in our own hearts.

Here are some markers that often accompany those who indulge in bad judgment.

**Pride.** Pride rears its ugly head when we compare ourselves to others and declare ourselves better than they are. In doing so, we lower the standard that God holds us to, which is perfection (Matthew 5:48). Since no one can live up to God's standard, holding ourselves to others' makes us feel better than we should. It's easier to say, "I'm not perfect, but at least I'm not like *them*," than to admit that "I'm not perfect, and I've got a lot of work to do on myself."

Pride runs rampant in politics, where everyone's looking to highlight what's wrong with the other party's candidates and ideas. Instead of looking inward and perfecting themselves, pride makes politicians throw stones at each other's glass houses. Pride fuels lowest-common-denominator politicking— a race to the bottom that sickens onlookers and candidates alike. And pride is what makes us hate politics the most— both the pride we see in others and that which is revealed in ourselves.

Scripture warns us that pride comes before the fall (see Proverbs 16:18), which we regularly see played out in the news. Politicians are more often felled by their own shortcomings than they are by better candidates or campaigns. That's because pride focuses them horizontally on public perception rather than vertically on God's. When politicians focus on how they're perceived by voters rather than on doing what's right, their lives and careers eventually collapse like the house of cards they've built.

**Hypocrisy.** Jesus had a zero-tolerance policy when it came to hypocrisy. He addressed it in the Sermon on the Mount, saying, "Why do you look at the speck of sawdust in your brother's eye and pay no attention to the plank in your own eye? . . . You hypocrite, first take the plank out of your own eye, and then you will see clearly to remove the speck from your brother's eye" (Matthew 7:3–5).

In these verses, Jesus reminds us that our own sin is always the greatest and to nip it in the bud before we start tackling others'. To which some might protest, "That can't possibly be true! I'm doing my best to live a godly life over here, while that person is flaunting her sin!"

From a human perspective, they might be right—someone who flagrantly sins could be considered a "bigger" sinner in that moment. But Jesus judges us by a very different standard—one that levels the playing field for all. Scripture says that "*all* have sinned and fall short of the glory of God" (Romans 3:23, emphasis added). There's nothing we can do to change that reality, as all our "righteousness" is like filthy rags to God (Isaiah 64:6). We are therefore equal in the weight of our sins, which God's grace alone saves us from.

**Superficiality.** Jesus says in John 7:24 to stop judging others by "mere appearances." As someone who invests time and energy in looking "put together," I really struggle with this teaching. It's hard to focus on what someone else is saying when I'm distracted by how they speak, look, and act.

We've all judged and been judged based on our outward packaging. But nowhere is culture, including the church, more culpable of judging people than based on their party affiliation. The names we call those we disagree with are both hateful and ignorant. By categorizing others a certain way, we allow ourselves to dismiss them outright. In doing so, we fail to understand *why* they believe what they do and miss out on important spiritual truths. Since Christians occupy both sides of the aisle, it's incumbent on us to listen and honor, rather than judge and diminish, our fellow believers' beliefs. By simply respecting their experiences and perspectives, we could do wonders to bridge our partisan divide.

Superficiality works against unity, but it also works against us as well. Proverbs 16:2 tells us that "all a person's ways seem pure to them, but motives are weighed by the Lord." So while we might think our motivations are pure because they seem that way to us, they could just as easily be selfish and wrong. As the "discerner of the thoughts and intents of the heart" (Hebrews 4:12 NKJV), God is never fooled. We should therefore ask Him to expose the superficiality in our own hearts by praying as the pslamist did: "Explore me, O God, and know the real me. *Dig deeply and discover who I am.* Put me to the test and watch how I handle the strain. *Examine me to* see if there is an evil bone in me and guide me down Your path forever" (Psalm 139:23–24 VOICE).

**Retaliation.** The Bible says, "Judge not, that ye be not judged" (Matthew 7:1 KJV) because everyone fears retaliation. The threat of being treated the way we treat others should nip our judgment in the bud. But rather than reject it, we weaponize it instead, trying to out-judge each other. It's a classic case of hurt people hurting people and perpetuating a cycle of abuse.

In the political context, this happens when someone throws the first punch and gets one in return. The one who first received the punch, however, often ups the ante. This feeds right into the golden rule of campaigning, which is to respond to anything negative with something equally or more negative about your opponent. Abiding by this rule facilitates a race to the bottom and fuels our hatred of politics.

The only way to break our retaliatory judgment cycle is by forgiving and letting God avenge the sin that's been committed against us. As candidates, voters, and people with opinions, we'll always be judged for expressing those opinions. But we can and must stop our downward civic spiral by refraining from judging in return. In doing so, we leave our reputations in God's hands and prove how much we trust Him.

The good news is that God is much better at avenging injustice than we could ever be. Scripture promises that in obeying His instruction to "bless those who curse [us]" (Luke 6:28), we'll "find favor and a good name in the sight of God and man" (Proverbs 3:4). He also promises that He'll restore what the locusts have eaten and give us a double portion for our trouble (Joel 2:25; Isaiah 61:7). Assurances like these help me forgive my offenders and put my retaliatory impulses to rest.

**Falsehood.** Being wrong is part and parcel of being human; hence the saying "to err is human."[7] No matter how wise we are, Paul tells us that we can only understand things "in part" on this side of heaven (1 Corinthians 13:12). Only God is omniscient; we are not. As such, we should think twice before judging others when our perspectives are limited.

This is true of our political opinions as well. In the free market of ideas, we're so focused on proving we're right that we often lose sight of the fact that we're all dealing with imperfect information. This isn't to say that there's no biblical distinction between right and wrong; there certainly is, and God makes that clear in Scripture. But the fact that both parties use Scripture to justify their positions means there can be more than one interpretation of the truth.

One way to avoid being labeled a know-it-all is to humbly acknowledge how little we actually know. This admission alone would change *everything* about the way we do politics. Acknowledging that we need more information to make better decisions would cause us to reach out to those we disagree with and solicit their input with gratitude. Abraham Lincoln did so to great effect in hiring a "team of rivals" to be his inner circle. His decision to do so reunited our country in the wake of the Civil War and proved the brilliance of Scripture: "Wisdom is found in those who take advice" (Proverbs 13:10) and "Victory is won through many advisors" (Proverbs 11:14).

**Fear.** Fear leads to bad judgment because it causes us to be more concerned with our own needs than we are about learning the truth. Like dogs suffering from fear aggression, people tend to lash out at others, thinking they can protect themselves against how they might be judged by striking first. Such anticipatory fear is selfish in nature and focused on protecting our own interests at the expense of others'. It also flies in the face of Scripture, which tells us to "seek the interests of others" even at the expense of our own (Philippians 2:4; 1 Corinthians 10:24).

According to psychologist Abraham Maslow's Hierarchy of Needs, we cannot love ourselves or others if our basic physiological, psychological, and relational needs are unmet. But according to the Gospel of Matthew, putting God and others first is not only possible, but required of believers, since God meets all of our needs himself. As Christians, our faith isn't in political parties or presidential candidates to protect or provide for our families. Rather, our faith is in *God*, who provides "immeasurably more than all we ask or imagine" (Ephesians 3:20).

Fear of man is anathema to faith in God. It causes us to give others power over our lives that only belongs to Him. Fear causes us to feel anxious, which prevents us from living the abundant life we've been promised (John 10:10). Thankfully, eliminating

152

our fear of man is as simple as reminding ourselves of the truth: that we have not been given the spirit of fear, "but of power and of love and of a sound mind" (2 Timothy 1:7 NKJV). Repeating this truth until I believe it helps me minimize fear's impact on my life and maximize my gratitude to God for being my protector and provider.

## A Family Affair

Now that we've established how to distinguish between good and bad judgment, the question turns to the very important point of *who* we are to judge. We all fall into the trap of judging those who believe and behave differently than we do. And sometimes we judge with a motivation of love, thinking that if we point out where they've gone wrong, we'll eventually lead them to truth.

But Scripture makes it crystal clear that we are only to judge those within the church. "What business is it of mine," Paul asked, "to judge those outside the church? Are you not to judge those inside?" (1 Corinthians 5:12). In the same way that children from other families can't be held to a standard of behavior that aligns with ours, we can only judge those who claim to be our siblings in Christ. "God," Paul assures us, "will judge those outside" (1 Corinthians 5:13), freeing us to love them without any judgment whatsoever.

## The Judgment Decision Tree

The decision of what, who, and how to judge boils down to the following.

First, does the person claim to be a Christian? If not, your only job is to pray for them and speak to any issues that may be harming them or others. This takes enormous restraint and a great deal of self-awareness to do right. If you find yourself doubting your motives for approaching them, I recommend defaulting to prayer instead. God can reach them in myriad ways, and He doesn't need your help making His point!

If the person *does* claim to be a Christian, pray about whether you're the right person to bring about correction. The answer is more likely to be yes if you're already in relationship with them and they know that you speak from a motivation of love. If not, pray about whether it's you or someone closer to them who's better suited to deliver the judgment.

If you're the person God chooses to use for correction, ask Him to reveal your motives, and purify them if necessary. This is where Christians get most confused about whether to address sin in another's life. We all accept that we have "sinned and fall short of the glory of God," and that we continue to sin as part of our human nature (Romans 3:23). Lest we consider ourselves holier than Paul, who confessed to sinning against his own will (Romans 7:15–20), we will all deal with sin until the day we die.

But should our own sin prevent us from exercising godly judgment toward others? A look at Paul's life as a missionary gives us a clear answer to this question. In spite of his own self-professed sin, Paul was an effective and loving disciplinarian of the many churches he planted. His letters to the Corinthians, Ephesians, and Romans were filled with life-giving advice and stern exhortations that addressed their sin from a place of love and concern. The question, then, isn't whether our personal sin should keep us from judging others—the answer to that, based on Paul's example, is an unequivocal *no*. Our decision as to whether to judge should hinge, instead, on whether our motives are pure. If our judgment is truly for the sake of others, rather than ourselves, then we have the green light to move on to other important considerations.

Next, we deal with the question of *how* to address sin in another's life. When it comes to speaking hard truths, Scripture instructs us to do so "in love" (Ephesians 4:15). This warning is both for our sake and theirs, since Scripture says that "with the judgment you pronounce you will be judged, and with the measure you use it will be measured to you" (Matthew 7:2 ESV). In other words, we're judged as harshly or lovingly as we judge others. We should therefore judge carefully, with an abundance of grace, to ensure that we receive the same treatment in return.

Finally, Matthew 18 details the proper way to address sin in another's life:

> If your brother or sister sins, go and point out their fault, just between the two of you. If they listen to you, you have won them over. But if they will not listen, take one or two others along, so that "every matter may be established by the testimony of two or three witnesses." If they still refuse to listen, tell it to the church; and if they refuse to listen even to the church, treat them as you would a pagan or a tax collector.
>
> Matthew 18:15–17

Matthew's instructions are clear as can be, offering a process that enables us to judge properly.

## Team Jesus

Most of us judge others based on their political beliefs, but Jesus says that our common faith overrides any differences we may perceive. Jesus taught this principle to the disciples when John tried to stop a man from driving demons out in Jesus' name. "We tried to stop him," John explained, "because he was not following us" (Mark 9:38 ESV). John and the disciples thought that anyone who wasn't one of them shouldn't do anything, including *heal* people, in Jesus' name.

Jesus' response must have surprised John: "Do not stop him . . . for whoever is not against us is for us" (Mark 9:39–40).

Jesus' point was that as long as we're on the same spiritual team, we have a common bond in Christ, which is stronger than any other affiliation in the world. The disciples may have been the only ones lucky enough to roll with Jesus, but that didn't mean His power and wisdom were limited to them. The Holy Spirit is equally accessible to everyone, and so is God's truth. It doesn't reside in one political party to the exclusion of another, or certain politicians over others. Acknowledging this is a big step toward getting our judgment right.

So let's take the "kick me" signs off of each other's backs and start treating each other like family instead. After all, we're on the same team, and none of us have this political stuff nailed. The godliest thing we can do is admit it, as doing so will allow a fuller picture of God's justice and truth to emerge.

Finally, let's stop shooting our wounded. When someone is caught in sin or proven to be patently wrong, let's call it what it is and love them back into the family. Like Jesus, we should all be full of both grace and truth, "for judgment is without mercy to one who has shown no mercy. Mercy triumphs over judgment" (James 2:13 ESV). Mercy makes it easier to view others the way God does: as family members rather than political enemies, empowered to solve our nation's problems together.

## REFLECTION

1. How do you judge people you disagree with, and what does that say about you?
2. Which sins keep you from judging well, and how can you address them in your life?
3. How could you reframe the way you think about those you disagree with so that you view them the way Jesus does: as family members rather than foes?

## PRAYER

*Lord, I struggle to judge others in a manner that is objective and life-giving rather than subjective and destructive. I have much to learn about judging well, and a lot of experience doing it wrong. Help me get this important skill right so that I can bring your truth into the political arena and use it to unify rather than divide the body of Christ. In Jesus' name, Amen.*

## 11

# LOVE YOUR ENEMIES

When you learn to sit at the table with Judas, you'll learn the love of Christ.

—Sarah Ann

Halfway through my congressional race, I got tired of running— not the exercise, but for office. I jumped into the race late in the cycle, so the whole thing was a flat-out sprint. The seven months between my campaign announcement and the primary election were the most grueling of my life. During those months, I experienced more backstabbing, name-calling, and reputational damage than anyone deserved. By the time I won the primary, even my victory felt like a defeat. The fact that I still had five months to go—and a richer and more powerful opponent to face in the general election—made me want to crawl back into bed rather than fight another day.

However, not wanting to appear weak or in any way defeated, I hid my exhaustion from everyone. Rather than fight my opponents head on, I deflected their punches or laughed them off. I pledged never to let anyone get the best of me, and on the outside, that's how it appeared. But underneath my confident façade was a seething, hardened woman.

After one particularly grueling debate, I yelled (in the privacy of my car), "*Who* do these people think they are?" I'd just gotten pummeled by my primary opponents, who'd struck a pact to take me out. Their attacks were constant and unrelenting. I refused to let them see me sweat, but their coordinated assaults were the straws that broke this camel's back. I went to bed pledging to destroy them, and a hatred for the entire campaign took root in my heart.

Moreover, it wasn't just my opponents who wore on me; nearly everyone did. It wasn't their fault—most just wanted to help. But every request they made demanded something of me that I had run out of energy to give. The steady drumbeat of media interviews, press events, Rotary Club meetings, and Soroptimist International breakfasts got me up early and kept me working late, seven days a week. It all felt like a grind rather than the blessing and privilege it was.

Even a good night's sleep couldn't shake me out of my disgruntled state. The only thing that elevated my mood was praying and running. So the morning after that brutal debate, I went for a run and chat with God. My daily route took me along the San Diego Harbor, which offered a view of the most beautiful parts of my district. Thirty minutes in, I stopped at the turnaround point to prepare myself for another exhausting day on the campaign trail. As I gazed out at Coronado Island and Point Loma, I could hardly focus on the beauty before me. All I felt was bitter and upset, and God got an earful that morning.

"*Why* is everyone coming after *me*, Lord? I feel like I have a perpetual target on my back. If it isn't one thing, it's another, and even my friends are starting to annoy me. Why is everyone so needy? Can't they see how busy I am doing *your* work?" I went on like this for at least ten minutes, and God let me continue until I paused to take a breath.

Suddenly, out of nowhere, the word *love* popped into my mind. *How random*, I thought . . . *love?* What did love have to do with my campaign? I was laser-focused on doing God's work and winning this race. Plus, I barely had time to love myself, much less think about loving others.

As quickly as these questions came to mind, God answered them. In my spirit, I heard Him say, "You're focused on all the wrong things, Denise. You're faking your love for others and trying to win at their expense. You're missing the whole point of why I called you to run in the first place. Your primary responsibility is to *love* people. I can't give you authority over that which you don't love. Only love qualifies you to lead."

My heart sank as God's admonition seared my conscience. By nature, I'm more transactional than relational, and winning is my MO. Over the course of the campaign, I'd gotten so wrapped up in winning "for God" that I'd unwittingly cast love to the wayside. And when I lost my love, I lost God's favor, because He could not bless anything I did apart from it.

Humbled and convicted, I asked God to refill me with love for friend and enemy alike. The more I prayed, the lighter my steps grew, and over the course of my run home, God changed my heart. By the time I walked through my apartment door, I was refilled with love for Him, myself, and others. And that made me a candidate whom God could finally use for His glory.

## Love in Action

The saying "Love is a verb, not a feeling" has always resonated with me. Growing up, I knew that I was loved because of the countless sacrifices my parents made on my behalf. Their hard work enabled me to be, do, and try anything I set my mind to. In my family, love looked like Dad taking on three jobs to pay for my extracurricular activities, and Mom shuttling me to and from swim meets; piano, dance, and horseback riding lessons; and Saturday morning Chinese school.

I, however, have a different way of expressing my love. On Gary Chapman's *Five Love Languages* test, I rate off the charts on words of affirmation. I used to think that meant I wasn't doing enough to show people I loved them, but it turns out that all five love languages—gift-giving, quality time, physical touch, acts of service, and words of affirmation—require some sort of action in order to be expressed.

Loving my family and friends with words of encouragement comes naturally to me. I want to be the person they can come to for a pep talk when they need one. But encouraging those I don't particularly like has always been much harder. I wouldn't say that I'm *intentionally* unloving toward those I disagree with. I'm just less inclined to go out of my way to find a reason to give them a verbal pat on the back.

I often wonder if the human side of Jesus ever felt the same way. There He was, God in a bod, living among a bunch of sinners. There were the obvious sinners, like murderous Saul-turned-Paul and dishonest tax-collecting Matthew; the less obvious sinners, like Peter the hot-headed fisherman and Thomas the perpetual doubter; and those who seemed to be perfect on the outside but sinned in their hearts, like the Pharisees. But while the first two categories of sinners were easier to love than the third, Jesus expressed His love toward all of them. His compassion was proactive, His actions intentional, and His words a salve for their broken and needy hearts. This was true of Jesus no matter who He interacted with, and no matter how they treated Him in return. As bestselling author Bob Goff says in a book title, Jesus loved *Everybody Always*. And as His followers, we are commanded and expected to do the same.

## What Is Love?

*Love* is one of the most overused words in America. I'm as guilty as everyone else in proclaiming my "love" for ice cream, puppies, and a great shoe sale when the only things I truly love are my family, my friends, and God. By diluting its significance, we demote love, making it ordinary, common, and *de minimis*— when in reality, it's anything but.

Love is described in Scripture as sacrificial, deferential, and long-suffering—not some warm and fuzzy feeling that flows out of us when we're happy and surrounded by people who fill us up. The kind of love Jesus displayed defied explanation. When mocked by His enemies, He prayed for their souls. When challenged by the Pharisees, He gave them every opportunity to repent and receive Him as Lord. When doubted by the weak, He helped their unbelief. And when crucified by the masses, He forgave them and asked His Father to do the same.

Jesus' actions redefined love and turned culture's definition upside down. Paul put what Jesus modeled into words, writing:

> Love is patient, love is kind. It does not envy, it does not boast, it is not proud. It does not dishonor others, it is not self-seeking, it is not easily angered, it keeps no record of wrongs. Love does not delight in evil but rejoices with the truth. It always protects, always trusts, always hopes, always perseveres.
>
> 1 Corinthians 13:4–7

Jesus commanded us to love only two things in this world— God and people. When He issued this commandment, there were over six hundred laws that religious Jews had to adhere to in order to be considered righteous before the Lord. Jesus boiled all of them down, including the Ten Commandments, to these two, declaring "the entire law and all the demands of the prophets" fulfilled through them (Matthew 22:40 NLT).

Moreover, these were *commandments*, meaning that these weren't mere suggestions, but heavenly decrees requiring proactive compliance on our part.

To all of the above, especially as it relates to politics, I'd reiterate that love is more than tolerance. Tolerance is a counterfeit for love; like a fake one-hundred-dollar bill, it appears the same until closer examination reveals its worthlessness. Tolerance is passive, requiring that we permit or allow certain things to happen around us. Love, on the other hand, is proactive, requiring risk and sacrifice for others. Tolerance is about letting things be rather than trying to make things better. Love is about restoring people and improving outcomes for everyone involved. Tolerance leads to apathy, indifference, and avoidance. Love, on the other hand, leads to connection, transformation, and unity.

Finally, the opposite of love isn't what most people think it is; it isn't hatred, but rather fear. That's why Scripture says, "There is no fear in love," and "perfect love drives out fear" (1 John 4:18). Hatred is a byproduct of fear, stemming from our deeply embedded survival instincts. But fear is what shrinks us inwardly and away from others, preventing us from loving them the way Jesus commanded us to.

## How Do We Love?

Jesus commands us to love both God and our neighbors, including our mortal enemies. And since it's easy to love the neighbors we feel affection for, most of His teachings center on how to love God as well as those we tend to hate.

Since God has no earthly form, it's hard to understand how to love Him. We can't see Him or touch Him, much less pull up a chair or come in for a hug. Thus, most denominations portray Him as a "father" rather than a "daddy," which makes us think of Him as a disciplinarian rather than a doting parent. It's no surprise, then, that so many of us would rather hide from God and are more inclined to fear Him than to show Him love.

It's only in the context of a personal relationship with God that we experience the "height, breadth, depth and width" of His love for us (Ephesians 3:17–19). And when we do, it's so much easier to respond to Him. As John says, it is not our job to initiate, but only to reciprocate: "We love [Him] because He first loved us" (1 John 4:19). Loving God is thus a natural response to being in relationship with Him. Knowing *how* to love God, however, is not.

Thankfully, Scripture teaches us how to love God: "And this is love: that we walk in obedience to his commands" (2 John 1:6). Obedience to His Word is how we express our love. There are myriad ways to obey God in Scripture, from giving to the poor, to fighting for justice, to spreading the gospel far and wide. These are just a sampling of the many areas in which God asks for our obedience, and we can express our love by responding affirmatively.

But Paul, as usual, takes it one step further by asking us to examine our motives. In his first letter to the Corinthians, Paul tells us that even if we do everything right in God's eyes, we gain nothing without love.

> If I speak in the tongues of men or of angels, but do not have love, I am only a resounding gong or a clanging cymbal. If I have the gift of prophecy and can fathom all mysteries and all knowledge, and if I have a faith that can move mountains, but do not have love, I am nothing. If I give all I possess to the poor and give over my body to hardship that I may boast, but do not have love, I gain nothing.
>
> 1 Corinthians 13:1–3

In these verses, Paul is saying that no matter how spiritual, sac-rificial, or "Christian" our obedience appears to be, none of it means anything to God if it's done with any motive other than love.

This is a hard pill for some, like me, to swallow. I'd rather go through the motions of doing loving things than invest my time and energy into actually loving those I hate. But apparently, doing spiritual things that most Christians would applaud gets me nowhere with the One I'm most eager to please. Obeying God requires more than just good works; it requires sacrificially loving our enemies.

While knowing that fuels my *desire* to love my enemies, it doesn't make *doing* so any easier. As hard as loving an unseen God is, loving a mean-spirited person is a million times harder. This reality was reflected in the prevailing theology of Jesus' day, which was to "hate forever the unjust."[1] Jesus' lesson on love was a radical departure from what His contemporaries taught: "You have heard that it was said, 'Love your neighbor and hate your enemy.' But I tell you, love your enemies and pray for those who persecute you, that you may be children of your Father in heaven" (Matthew 5:43–45).

It's one thing to tolerate someone else's shenanigans. It's another thing to love those who are dangerous, wicked, and cruel. And yet, that's exactly how Jesus taught His audience to respond to their enemies, which the story of the Good Samaritan illustrates.

## The Good Samaritan, Revisited

In the book of Luke, a lawyer asked Jesus to define what He meant by the word *neighbor*. The lawyer was looking for a loophole in Jesus' definition. But rather than respond to the lawyer directly, Jesus answered him with the following parable:

A man was going down from Jerusalem to Jericho, and he fell among robbers, who stripped him and beat him and departed, leaving him half dead. Now by chance a priest was going down that road, and when he saw him he passed by on the other side. So likewise a Levite, when he came to the place and saw him, passed by on the other side. But a Samaritan, as he journeyed, came to where he was, and when he saw him, he had compassion. He went to him and bound up his wounds, pouring on oil and wine. Then he set him on his own animal and brought him to an inn and took care of him. And the next day he took out two denarii and gave them to the innkeeper, saying, "Take care of him, and whatever more you spend, I will repay you when I come back."

Luke 10:30–35 ESV

At that point, Jesus turned back to the lawyer, asking "'Which of these three, do you think, proved to be a neighbor to the man who fell among the robbers?' He said, 'The one who showed him mercy.' And Jesus said to him, 'You go, and do likewise.'" (Luke 10:36–37).

While there's plenty to unpack in this story, there are three main points that speak to what loving our neighbor really means.

**First, love pays attention.** In researching this story, I learned a surprising fact: the first two men who crossed the street and looked the other way were both in ministry. One was a priest, and the other a Levite, both of whom served their local churches. Given their vocational choices, both were likely good and godly men. However, their priorities were off; by crossing the street and ignoring the man in need, they showed that they cared more about doing "religious" things than loving their fellow countryman.

Meanwhile, the Samaritan, an avowed enemy of the hurting Judean, did what no one else would: he paid attention to him. He literally stopped in the middle of his own journey, bound up the stranger's wounds, dressed them, put him on his own donkey, took him to an inn, and cared for him personally. The next day, he paid for his room, board, and medical expenses, instructed the innkeeper to care for him, and offered to cover the remaining bill upon his return. The Samaritan dropped everything he was doing and gave of his own time and money to prioritize a man who was, in every sense of the word, his mortal enemy.

**Second, love bridges division.** Our hero was particularly controversial to those in Jesus' audience because Jews and Samaritans hated each other for centuries. Their enmity stemmed from political and religious division among the tribes of Jacob and devolved into national and racial differences later. Imagine Catholics and Protestants in Northern Ireland, Sunnis and Shiites in the Middle East, Democrats and Republicans in America, then multiply all that antipathy by ten. That's how much these people groups hated each other.

The Good Samaritan broke every social norm by helping the hurting Judean. Though there were plenty to choose from, he didn't allow any excuses to prevent him from helping his enemy. He could have easily crossed the street like the others—and the Judean may have preferred that to being helped by a Samaritan. But instead of turning his back on his enemy, the Samaritan nursed him back to life and bridged their division with love.

**Third, love is costly.** In telling this parable, Jesus details every action the Samaritan took for a reason: He wants us to recognize the high price the Samaritan paid to care for his enemy. In terms of time, he spent a whole day and night caring for the Judean. He could have easily paid someone else to do it or left the innkeeper to care for him overnight, but instead he took the responsibility on himself.

In terms of money, the two denarii he gave the innkeeper were equivalent to two days' wages—a considerable amount to give anyone, much less an enemy. Those two denarii would have covered the man's stay for two months' room and board. Moreover, the Samaritan pledged to pay any additional expenses the stranger incurred—without asking the innkeeper to return any amount that wasn't used.

Jesus used these details to underscore His point: loving an enemy often requires personal sacrifice. Given that Jesus paid the ultimate price to love His enemies, He speaks with authority on this matter when asking us to do the same.

## Love and Politics

At the end of the story, Jesus instructs the lawyer to "go and do likewise" (Luke 10:37). This is a directive to the lawyer and all of us as well. While we may not stumble across a mugged Judean, we constantly cross paths with people we'd consider our enemies who are in emotional, financial, physical, and spiritual pain. Their pain often expresses itself in political outrage, which contributes to our division. But by tending to their pain like the Samaritan did, we can help bridge our division with love.

Other ways that we can express our love in politics include the following.

**Speak His truth.** One of the many ways that we can obey God is by speaking His truth in love (Ephesians 4:15). I'll elaborate more on this principle later, but for now, I want to make the point that Christians could revolutionize politics by championing kingdom principles over partisan platforms. Currently, most Americans are consumed with picking a side and defending it with their lives. But speaking God's truth, which at some point will likely conflict with our chosen side's politics, is still the best way to honor God and our neighbors.

**Redefine your enemy.** Most of us define our political enemies as people we disagree with. Yet Scripture tells us that in any struggle, "We do not wrestle against flesh and blood," but "against the spiritual forces of evil in the heavenly places" (Ephesians 6:12 ESV). When people come against us, it isn't *them* consciously doing so, but rather the *spiritual forces* controlling them. Thus, our enemies aren't people, but rather the one who divides us.

The devil's primary mission on earth is to "steal and kill and destroy" (John 10:10) God's people. Since unity is so important to God, Satan loves to weaponize us against each other. Doing so is his attempt to divide and conquer the body of Christ. Therefore, the best way to defeat him is by directing our anger at the devil himself. Praying *against* evil and *for* "those who persecute" us (Matthew 5:44) focuses us on defeating our common enemy rather than each other.

**Bless your enemies.** In Luke 6:27–28, Jesus says, "Love your enemies, do good to those who hate you, bless those who curse you, pray for those who mistreat you." In other words, do the opposite of what your enemies do to you, "without expecting to get anything back" (Luke 6:35).

On its face, there doesn't seem to be any benefit to obeying Jesus' words. Revenge is sweet for a reason—it feels good getting people back for the evil they've done to us, at least in the short term. In the long term, however, treating our enemies poorly actually hurts us more than it does them. That's why Scripture tells us to bless our enemies and adds a money-back guarantee: "Bless those who persecute you; bless and do not curse. . . . Do not repay anyone evil for evil. . . . Do not take revenge, my dear friends, but leave room for God's wrath, for it is written: 'It is mine to avenge; I will repay,' says the Lord" (Romans 12:14, 17, 19). I'm not saying we should only bless our enemies so that God can repay them for the harm they've caused, but it sure feels like an added benefit that makes blessing them worthwhile!

## What's Really at Stake

Given how vitriolic politics are today, they're the ultimate testing ground for love. I'm convinced that if we figure out how to love in the political context, we can get it right in almost any other aspect of our lives.

There are so many reasons why we must, the most important one being our witness. The world is watching those of us who call ourselves Christians to determine if Jesus is actually real. By obeying His Word and loving our enemies, we show them a supernatural way of living that makes the world sit up and take notice. .

The only tangible relationship we have with Christ is the one we have with each other. How we treat those God has called us to love is a direct reflection of our love for Him. When we tear each other down, we tear Christ down; the two cannot be separated. Thus, the way we treat each other here and now has earthly and eternal consequences, a truth we must remain cognizant of when engaging in the political realm.

## REFLECTION

1. How good are you at loving others even when you don't feel loving toward them?
2. What price are you willing to pay to love your enemies?
3. What steps can you take today to love your enemies—political or otherwise?

## PRAYER

*Lord, I fall so far short in loving people, especially those I dislike. My instinct is never to love first, but to argue, fight, and win. Override my human instincts with your supernatural love, and open my eyes to see that Satan is our real enemy. Help me express your love, in politics and in life, as a testimony of your power and truth. In Jesus' name, Amen.*

# SPEAKING TRUTH IN LOVE

*Truth without love is brutality and love without truth is hypocrisy.*
—Warren Wiersbe

As both a lawyer and a Christian, I'm used to jokes being made at my expense. One of my favorites is an oldie but a goodie that pastors use to warm up a crowd:

A man arrives at the gates of heaven. St. Peter asks, "Religion?"
The man says, "Methodist."
St. Peter looks down his list and says, "Go to Room 24, but be very quiet as you pass Room 8."
Another man arrives at the gates of heaven. "Religion?"
"Lutheran."
"Go to Room 18 but be very quiet as you pass Room 8."
A third man arrives at the gates. "Religion?"
"Presbyterian."
"Go to Room 11 but be very quiet as you pass Room 8."

The man says, "I can understand there being different rooms for different denominations, but why must I be quiet when I pass Room 8?"

St. Peter tells him, "Well, the Baptists are in Room 8, and they think they're the only ones here."

This joke elicits chuckles because we all know it's true. Substitute any denomination for the four above, and it still works just as well. As a "Bapti-costal-terian" with a strong affinity for Jesuits, I have dabbled with more denominations than most. And every denomination I've ever encountered secretly believes that *they* are the narrow road that *truly* leads to life (Matthew 7:13–14).

The desire to be on the right side of both heaven and history are two reasons that religious and political folks are so divided. And our interest in aligning with God's truth is a noble and virtuous one. But many have ditched humility and honor while championing their versions of reality, making God's truth more divisive than it ought to be.

## "The Truth Hurts!"

I've never had a problem with telling anyone my version of the truth. Both of my parents are outspoken in their beliefs, and they raised me to be the same. My teenage years were predictably tumultuous, given that my "truths" differed so much from theirs. Sometimes our differences got out of control, and my mom would say something mean. When she did, she rarely apologized, and often doubled down. "Honey," she'd say, with no regret, "the truth hurts—deal with it!" I internalized her words and gave myself a license to say whatever I wanted—hurting people and expecting them to thank me for setting them straight!

For the record, my mom and I no longer talk or think this way. Both of us have since matured, in age as well as faith. When we chose to follow Jesus and submit our wills to Him, the Holy Spirit tamed our tongues and checked our pride. We did not, however, give up on truth-telling. If anything, God made us *more* emboldened to speak truth. The difference is that we now do so from a position of love.

## Love Is Truthful

God commands us to love each other, but not in the way culture defines love. Culture says that love is a feeling and our acceptance of others' "truths" is proof of our love. But Scripture says that love is a decision coupled with action, rooted in God's truth. Real love does not exist apart from His truth. We must therefore reflect both in equal measure.

In the book of Ephesians, Paul tells us to "speak the truth in love" (Ephesians 4:15). The love that he refers to is *agape* love, which seeks the best and highest good of others, often at our own expense. We learn to express agape love by following the example of Christ, who sacrificed himself to speak the truth for the sake of our salvation.

Paul instructs us to speak this way so that we can "become in every respect the mature body of him who is the head, that is, Christ" (Ephesians 4:15). Maturity enables us to recognize and choose good over bad, right over wrong, and life over death. And when we share God's truth in love, we help others make better choices too.

## Love Is Loving

As Christians, we don't get to simply define love as truth and call it a day. The *way* we express God's truth is *as* important as what we say. Expressing hard truths lovingly is the biggest challenge we all face. And nowhere is this more challenging than in today's political environment.

You'd think that with the emphasis Scripture puts on love, Christians would be best at showing it. But sadly, that has not been my experience with religion or politics. Christians are often just as mean as their secular counterparts. This is true even within my own friend group.

One morning during a recent election year, I met a friend for breakfast in Beverly Hills. This friend of mine is easily the most generous and Christlike person I know. She's always looking for ways to meet other people's needs and is a well-respected leader in our community. She also has strong opinions about politics and isn't afraid to express them.

While we laughed and chatted about life and God over fluffy pancakes and lattes, her sunny demeanor suddenly darkened. "What's wrong?" I asked, wondering what had caused her mood to shift. She responded to me by pointing at the front entrance of the restaurant. A politician she thoroughly disliked had just walked through it with his family.

"I'm gonna march over there right now and give him a piece of my mind," she said, grabbing the napkin off her lap and throwing it on her plate. I looked at her and felt taken aback, as this was completely out of character for her. I could tell she wasn't joking since she'd already pushed her chair back from the table.

My momentary shock gave way to a verse that suddenly came to mind. "A fool gives full vent to his spirit, but a wise man quietly holds it back" (Proverbs 29:11 ESV). I grabbed her hand as she turned to leave and asked her to sit back down. She looked at me, clearly miffed and frustrated by my restraint. "Don't you think he's absolutely ruining *everything*?" she asked, as if holding her back put me in cahoots with his political agenda.

"You know that I'm in total agreement with everything you're feeling right now. But I can't let you ruin his morning by yelling at him and scaring his kids. This isn't the right place, way, or time to express your frustrations," I said. "You're going to regret doing this—please sit back down."

She looked at me as if I'd slapped her clear across the face. "*Why* would I regret telling him exactly what's on my mind? He clearly needs somebody to tell him the truth. God hates what he's doing, and he needs a wake-up call. This is for *his* sake, as much as it is for mine."

"Listen, I know your heart for justice and truth, and that you're trying to do what's right. But even if you speak the truth to him, God wants you to do it in love. And love is the furthest motivation I sense from you right now."

She looked away, and I thought for a moment that she might start yelling at me instead. But to my relief, she sat back down, looking very conflicted. "I'm just so frustrated with how his politics are ruining our children and lives," she said. "And I feel like I need to do my part to protect my family from him."

Jesus dealt with a similar situation when Peter rushed to his defense. When Jesus was arrested, Peter drew his sword and cut off Malchus's ear (John 18:10). He did so thinking he could save Jesus from being dragged away and killed. Peter's actions were motivated by loyalty and love. But Jesus rebuked Peter, telling him to put his sword away (John 18:11). Jesus then undid the damage that Peter had done to Malchus's ear (Luke 22:51). Rather than attack His enemies, Jesus showed them love.

Like my godly, feisty friend, Peter must have felt deflated at first. Here he was, thinking he was doing the right thing, standing up for Jesus. Wasn't putting his life on the line proof of his loyalty and commitment to truth? But as this story shows, Jesus values love as much as He does the truth. His commandment to love our enemies applies to everyone, all the time.

## The Four-Way Test

While running for Congress, I met with every single Rotary club in my district. Over time, I noticed that each Rotary club hung the same banner from its podium. On it was printed the "Four-Way Test," which read:

1. Is it the truth?
2. Is it fair to all concerned?
3. Will it build goodwill and better friendships?
4. Will it be beneficial to all concerned?

After my third Rotary speech, I asked my hosts to explain the purpose of this test. They said that it reminded their members to aim for the highest moral and ethical standards in their personal and professional lives. Intrigued, I looked up the history of the test and discovered that it was originally developed by a man who asked God for advice on how to turn a struggling business around. He knew that if his employees thought right, then they'd be more likely to act right too. So he prayed for God to give him an ethical yardstick that would help guide them into right conduct. After praying, he reached for a white paper card. He then wrote down the list above, which became the most widely printed statement of business ethics in the world.[1]

We desperately need a similar test in politics today. Imagine if candidates checked everything they said against the Four-Way Test. How differently would they speak and treat each other if they considered the impact of their actions and words? By putting the welfare of our nation ahead of their own selfish interests, they'd change the way politics are perceived and turn our struggling country around.

Regardless of whether that ever happens, I've adopted a version of this test in my own life. It's now my ethical yardstick for personal and professional relationships, as well as political engagement.

## Applying the Test to Politics

### 1. Is it factually true, in totality and principle?

In today's environment, where everyone's own version of truth is widely accepted as "true," there's no cultural standard for objective truth. The first thing we must therefore ask ourselves is whether our truth is, in fact, true.

One of the things that makes God, God is the fact that He's omniscient. Even the most spiritual among us "only know in part" (1 Corinthians 13:9–12) because only God knows all. Since truth is only partially known by even the wisest among us, we should humble ourselves and ask God to help us understand His whole truth. Part of that process is recognizing how influenced we are by our upbringing and environment. Where we're born, what our parents believe, and the color of our skin—all of these and many other factors contribute to our understanding of truth. This reality is reflected in the various ways that Christians vote. What else explains why 85% of white evangelicals vote Republican, while 90% of black Christians consistently vote for Democrats?[2]

One of the ways I seek more truth is by asking questions of those who share my faith but vote differently than I do. By asking honest questions, I can better understand how others' experiences have shaped their perspectives of God's truth. Their stories may not change my own opinions, but they do help me appreciate theirs. We may still agree to disagree, but we can do so with honor when we understand each other better.

The other question we must consider is whether our truths are rooted in the full truth of God as established in Scripture. In politics we're prone to cherry-picking the truths we stand behind. Consequently, Christians on both sides of the aisle have plenty of scriptural ammunition for their differing beliefs. However, neither party captures the full truth of God through a narrow partisan lens.

The best way I've discovered to counter this tendency is to keep a running list of all the things that God says He cares about. From justice to orphans and widows, to immigrants and the poor, to righteousness, life, and freedom, to holiness and family, God speaks plainly throughout Scripture as to what He loves and hates. By keeping a list, I'm reminded that my own interests are rarely the same as God's, and that honoring God means honoring *all* His interests, regardless of my partisan inclinations.

### 2. Is it fair to all involved, including those I disagree with?

In many people's minds, fairness is giving people exactly what they deserve. This definition, however, ignores the fact that God flipped the script on what's "fair" by showing us mercy and grace to spare us from what we deserve. Thus, our definition of fairness should be influenced more by grace than how the world tells us to treat each other.

Jesus' parable about the unforgiving servant illustrates how He expects us to treat others: A servant owed the king ten thousand talents that he couldn't pay back. So he begged for mercy, and the king obliged by canceling his debt. The servant then met a fellow servant who owed him a hundred denarii. He demanded payment and had his fellow servant thrown in prison when he could not pay.

When the king heard about this, he called for the first servant. "'You wicked servant,' he said, 'I canceled all that debt of yours because you begged me to. Shouldn't you have had mercy on your fellow servant just as I had on you?'" (Matthew 18:32–33). This parable is meant to remind us that we are all beneficiaries of God's unmerited grace, and that we should extend the same mercy to others that we have been shown.

Simply put, treating others fairly requires us to treat people better than they deserve. None of us deserves God's forgiveness, and someone you know may not deserve yours. God doesn't care either way; we are commanded to be merciful, regardless of our circumstances. Fair treatment, according to Scripture, means loving people and treating them honorably—even when they don't deserve it nor reciprocate in kind.

### 3. Will it build goodwill with all, and help me foster unity?

Matthew's Gospel clearly specifies how God wants us to treat each other: "Love your enemies, bless them that curse you, do good to them that hate you, and pray for them which despitefully use you, and persecute you" (Matthew 5:44 KJV). This verse isn't Jesus' best effort to turn us into martyrs, but rather to make us worthy of being called "children of God" (Matthew 5:45).

Some describe this kind of love as "unconquerable benevolence, invincible goodwill,"[3] which seeks the highest good of others. It's considered "unconquerable" because it has nothing to do with our feelings. Rather, it's a choice rooted in our free will—which is why we call it "goodwill" and not "good feelings." Goodwill overcomes feelings of offense, anger, and retaliation. It motivates us to love our enemies rather than react to the negative feelings they've caused.

In these verses, Jesus lists three ways that people show their ill will toward each other. *Cursing* means verbally denigrating others and destroying their reputations. *Hatred* is an active feeling of passionate antipathy toward another. *Spitefully using and persecuting* means taking advantage of and abusing someone unfairly.

To overcome these three hateful actions, Jesus gives us three ways to respond in love. We can *bless* those who curse us, meaning we can wish them well and return good words for their bad. We can *do good* to our enemies by serving them rather than retaliating. And we can *pray* for our enemies' welfare by asking God to protect and bless them. Each of these acts fosters goodwill, even if a two-way lovefest never materializes.

This is a major test for God's children who claim to want unity. By extending an olive branch when we'd rather retaliate, we "maintain the unity of the spirit in the bond of peace" (Ephesians 4:3 ESV). And while goodwill may not be appreciated by those we show it to, our heavenly Father sees and blesses us for it.

### 4. Will it be beneficial to all concerned, including my political "enemies"?

Our government was established to serve the interests of all Americans. As the Declaration of Independence clearly states, "all men are created equal," and "endowed by their Creator with certain unalienable Rights," including "Life, Liberty, and the pursuit of Happiness."[4]

However, this is not the mindset we take with us to the ballot box today. Campaigns are specifically designed to pit our interests against others'. Republicans are seen as siding with big business, free markets, churches, and traditional values, while Democrats are considered allies of big government, regulations, unions, and progress. Given that politics are positioned by parties as a zero-sum game, we're forced to pit ourselves against those in the opposite camp. We mistakenly believe that a win for "them" is an inevitable loss for "us," rather than recognizing that a rising tide lifts all boats.

Scripture, however, tells us a different story than what we're led to believe: that *God* is Jehovah Jireh, our Source and Provider. Governments may influence the quality of our lives, but God takes care of our needs. Believing this enables us to treat each other the way Paul urges us to: "Do nothing out of selfish ambition or vain conceit. Rather, in humility value others above yourselves, not looking to your own interests but each of you to the interests of the others" (Philippians 2:3–4).

Imagine if Christians led this way in politics today. Rather than backstabbing, slandering, or shutting down those we disagreed with, listening to, loving, and meeting their needs would turn politics on its head. Our influence would grow as a natural result of putting others first, and we would treat each other as allies rather than enemies.

## Internal Checklist

It's taken me decades to figure out how to speak the truth in love. I haven't perfected it, and I still make mistakes, but running through this checklist has been helpful.

### 1. Check your motives.

The book of Proverbs tells us that "all a person's ways seem pure to them, but motives are weighed by the Lord" (Proverbs 16:2). We can easily fool ourselves into thinking that our motives are purer than they actually are, especially when we think we're helping others. But too often, the truth is, we just want to win and be right.

There are two fail-proof ways to ensure that our motives are pure. The first is checking how we feel as we're gearing up to speak. If we're more focused on correcting someone than loving them back into the fold, then we're probably more interested in being right than delivering truth in love. The second is asking the Holy Spirit to convict us when we go off course. Being disciplined by God rarely feels good, but His correction is life-giving and beneficial. While it may sting in the moment, eventually we'll thank Him for it.

### 2. Read the room.

Before you dive into truth-telling, make sure you know your audience. What may come across as loving to some may be very unkind to others. That shouldn't change the substance of your message, but it should influence how you broach it. Ask the Lord to sensitize you to others and give you the right words to say in every room you're in.

In addition to considering your audience and message, think about timing and setting. When and where we speak our truths determines whether we shame or honor others. If our truth-speaking is done primarily on a public platform, such as social media or a stage, then it's probably motivated by self-interest and virtue signaling rather than a sincere love for others.

### 3. Seek to understand before seeking to be understood.

Most people tend to speak *about*, rather than *to*, those they disagree with. That's because people are generally uninterested in what other people think, or too focused on their own agenda to learn about others'.

God, however, cares about everything we think and feel. His concern stems from His love for us, which He commands us to extend to others. Seeking to understand another's perspective affirms their value and worth. By listening and learning, we express our respect for who they are and what they believe.

We don't have to agree with others just because we listen to them. But seeking to truly understand others is a practical way of conveying God's love. Speaking to, rather than about, those we disagree with helps us avoid unintentional misunderstandings. It also keeps us from gossiping, which Scripture strongly condemns (Proverbs 16:28; Ephesians 4:29; 1 Timothy 5:13).

### 4. Check your tongue.

A surefire indicator that someone's about to say something rude is the question, "Can I be honest?" These words make us feel self-defensive against anyone who utters them. And once we feel that way, it's hard to receive what they have to say.

Difficult truths must still be said, and it's hard to say them right. That's because our tongues seem to have minds of their own. The book of James warns us that the tongue can set "the

184

whole course of one's life on fire" (3:6). And the book of Proverbs tells us that the power of life and death is in the words we speak (18:21). Checking our tongues is therefore critical to speaking the truth in love. And while that is no easy feat, the Holy Spirit is ready and willing to help us tame our tongues.

By turning Ephesians 4:29 into a prayer, I've given the Lord free rein to shape what He wants me to say: "Let no unwholesome talk come out of my mouth, but only what is helpful for building others up according to their needs, that it may benefit those who listen." When I pray these words, I ask God to use me as His mouthpiece. That makes it far likelier that the words I say will be well-received by those who hear them.

### 5. Trust God to work it out.

You can't make anyone understand where you're coming from or make them want to change. But that's okay because our responsibility begins and ends in obedience. By speaking the truth in love, we fulfill the role God wants us to play. The heavy lifting of changing the listener's heart is a job for the Holy Spirit.

Hurt feelings and fractured relationships may well result from speaking the truth. We can hedge against this possibility by following this rule of thumb: the harder the truths, the greater the love, no matter who you're talking to. Speaking hard truths with an extra measure of love can go a long way to softening a blow.

Jesus was crucified for speaking truth in love, proving that total obedience to both principles does not protect us from suffering for it. Jesus warned us that in this world, following Him would cause us trouble (John 16:33). But as believers, we should worry less about our troubles and more about our souls. Jesus taught us that we shouldn't fear "those who kill the body but are unable to kill the soul; but rather fear Him who is able to destroy both soul and body in hell" (Matthew 10:28 NASB).

Obedience should thus be our primary focus, regardless of how daunting our adversaries may be. Doing our best and letting God do the rest is the beginning and end of our responsibility.

## REFLECTION

1. How committed are you to discerning the truth that God wants you to share?
2. What do you value more than truth that keeps you from speaking it boldly?
3. How loving are you when speaking hard truths, and how can you improve?

## PRAYER

*Lord, I'm admittedly bad at speaking your truth in love. It's a delicate balance and one that I end up falling on either side of too often. Help me discern more of your truth, and give me a greater measure of love. Guard my mouth, check my motives, and purify my heart so that your life-giving truth, spoken through me, transforms our nation for the better. In Jesus' name, Amen.*

## 13

# DIVE IN

You may not be interested in politics, but politics is interested in you.

—My spin on Fannie Hurst's quote about war

"I have no idea how you do it, Denise . . . I literally *hate* politics."

If I had a dollar for every time I heard some version of this statement, I'd have retired a long time ago. From friends to strangers, everyone has a response to what I do for a living. I get it—politics aren't something people are neutral about these days. They either think I'm great because they share my convictions, or they think I'm crazy, evil, and/or masochistic for being as involved as I am. The latter group generally falls into the "hating politics" camp, and given the title of my book, that likely includes you.

My hope in this chapter is to convince you that no matter how you feel about politics, there are plenty of reasons for you to dive in. And if you're a *Christian* reading this book, there are even *more* reasons why you actually *must*.

## The Case for Engagement

Most Americans ignore politics for myriad reasons. As Alexis de Toqueville noted in *Democracy in America*, it's primarily our desire to be left alone that causes us to steer clear of civic engagement. Our "American individualism" is "a reflective and quiet sentiment that inclines each individual to distance himself [and] build his own private world, willingly leaving the larger world to itself."[1] But when Americans leave leading to "others," we make ourselves vulnerable to those who assume power and leverage it for their own benefit. Our inclination toward "American individualism" is, moreover, anathema to our responsibilities as citizens.

A recent poll reveals another reason Americans are loath to get involved: they *hate* the division it causes between them and those they love. Two-thirds of respondents across party lines said that they planned to avoid talking politics with family and friends over Thanksgiving dinner.[2] Politics have become so toxic that they've turned our favorite holidays into relational land mines, prompting a DC-based media outlet to publish a guide titled "How to talk about politics with family this Thanksgiving."[3]

And yet, politics affect us all—whether or not we willingly engage. I personally invite hundreds of people to political events all year 'round, and it's always those who are "too busy" to attend who complain the most about our leadership. I laugh and ask, "How will things change if you don't get involved?" But many still choose to stay on the sidelines. I'm hoping that they'll eventually realize that it's impossible to be disengaged and unaffected. We can bury our heads deep in the sand, but we cannot hide from politics.

## The Case for *Christian* Engagement

For Christians, the case for civic engagement is even more compelling. The Gospel applies to every aspect of our lives, and the Bible gives us clear instruction regarding governmental and political authority. God himself created the government and calls those He puts in power "ministers of God" (Romans 13:6 ESV). He instructs us to submit ourselves "for the Lord's sake to every human institution, whether to a king as the one in authority, or to governors as sent by him" (1 Peter 2:13–14 NASB).

Throughout the Bible, we are told to steward the opportunities and blessings that God entrusts us with (Colossians 3:23; 1 Peter 4:10; 1 Corinthians 4:2). Since voting is a matter of stewardship, those who are blessed to live in a country where we can influence our government should vote and engage in a manner that both honors God and advances their neighbors' welfare.

Theologian Wayne Grudem reminds us that our engagement always makes a difference, for "when [the gospel] is truly proclaimed, [it] will result in changed lives. And I think Jesus wants us to have . . . changed schools, and changed neighborhoods and changed businesses and workplaces, and . . . changed governments."[4] As proof, he highlights the positive influence Christians have historically had on their countries. In the Roman Empire, Christians influenced their government to outlaw infanticide, child abandonment, abortion, and brutal gladiatorial contests. Christian influence caused the Indian government to prohibit the burning alive of widows with their dead husbands. Christian parliamentarian William Wilberforce ended the slave trade in England. And in China, Christians helped ban the painful practice of binding young women's feet. These changes occurred because "Christians realized that if they could influence laws and governments for good, they would be loving their neighbors as themselves, and they would be doing what Jesus said in Matthew 5:16."[5] Political involvement is therefore very much a part of living out our faith.

Scripture itself is filled with stories of how godly leaders leveraged their political influence. Three of my personal favorites include Joseph, Daniel, and Esther.

Joseph's story is a "pit to palace" tale. When Joseph was young, God prophesied his destiny as a leader. This caused his brothers to sell him into slavery to ensure that would never come to pass. But Joseph's integrity made him a standout in everything he did. Eventually he earned Pharaoh's trust and was appointed governor of Egypt. While in office, Joseph mandated the storage of food surpluses to prepare the nation for famine. His wisdom and foresight spared his country from starving to death, and God used Joseph's access and influence to spare his own family as well (Genesis 37, 39–45).

Daniel rose to power as a Jewish exile who was captured under King Nebuchadnezzar of Babylon. He was educated in the king's court and renamed Belteshazzar, meaning "Bel protects his life"—Bel being the god of the Babylonians. Despite his full-on Babylonian immersion, Daniel stayed true to the God of Israel. He blessed the king by interpreting his dreams and was appointed chief of all things supernatural (Daniel 5:11). Daniel's influence increased when he was thrown into a lion's den for refusing to worship other gods. When Daniel emerged alive and unscathed, King Darius issued an astounding decree "to all the nations and peoples of every language in all the earth . . . that in every part of [his] kingdom people must fear and reverence the God of Daniel" (Daniel 6:25–26). In total, Daniel served eight consecutive kings as both a government official and a prophet, blessing them all by directing them to the one true God.[6]

The book of Esther tells the story of a Jewish beauty who got the final rose in King Xerxes' season of *The Bachelor*. She then saved his life by warning of a murderous plot against him, which her uncle Mordecai had overheard and shared with her. Haman, the highest of all nobles, seethed with anger when Mordecai refused to bow before him. Haman plotted to hang anyone who refused to bow before anyone other than the Lord. So Esther stepped in and saved both her uncle and her people by leveraging her position and influence as queen. Her success led to Haman's demise, which prevented her husband from carrying out a state-sanctioned genocide of the Jewish people.

These are just three of many examples in the Bible of how godly people positively influenced a nation, its people, and its history. And now it's up to each of us to make a contribution worthy of our calling.

## To Whom Much Is Given

Scripture itself indicates why political participation is important. Luke 12:48 reads, "From everyone who has been given much, much will be demanded; and from the one who has been entrusted with much, much more will be asked." This verse has personal significance for me, as a first-generation American born of immigrant parents. My mother escaped the Communist regime, but much of her family did not. Those who were stuck behind were forced to relinquish their faith in God and replace it with faith in their government. Freedoms of speech, religion, and thought were banished by the Chinese Communist Party in an effort to keep the Chinese people under their leaders' control.

I experienced this firsthand when I was a missionary in China. Chinese Christians were forced underground to worship in hiding, and anyone deemed too sold-out to Jesus "disappeared" at the hands of government officials. Cameras were installed in hotel rooms to keep a watchful eye on foreigners, and any mention of historical events that conflicted with the government's account was banned from public discourse. While there, I was detained by government officials for showing the *Jesus* film. As I was being interrogated, I begged God to get me safely home. I was never happier than when they returned my passport and put me on the next flight to America. When I finally landed, I literally kissed the ground and thanked God for my country.

Until that moment, I'd never fully appreciated the freedoms associated with being an American. I'd taken for granted our ability to speak freely, to worship God publicly, and to disagree with the governmental powers that be. Being threatened for my beliefs, and sharing them with others, changed my life forever. This experience was a major catalyst for getting me involved in politics. I resolved that year to do all I could to preserve our blessed freedoms—to worship, think, speak, and live however God leads.

## Engage in Prayer

The first step I took to engage politically was praying for our governmental leaders. As I turned to the Bible for guidance, I stumbled onto Paul's first letter to Timothy. In it, Paul wrote, "I urge, then, first of all, that petitions, prayers, intercession and thanksgiving be made for all people—for kings and all those in authority, that we may live peaceful and quiet lives in all godliness and holiness. This is good, and pleases God our Savior" (1 Timothy 2:1–3). His instruction is clear, and his rationale apparent: praying for leaders pleases God because it helps align their wills with His.

Praying for our government also makes practical sense for those who are subject to it. Governments have significant control over churches, cities, and schools. It therefore behooves us to influence them by praying for God's will for our government, which allows us to freely follow God's will in our own lives.

The prophet Jeremiah established this principle when he told exiled Israelites to pray for the welfare of Babylon. "In its welfare, you will find your welfare" (Jeremiah 29:7 ESV)—and sure enough, they did. Within a few years of being conquered, some Israelites grew prosperous enough to buy massive tracts of land. Others rose to prominence as royal merchants, courtiers, and officials in direct service to the king. The Jewish King Jehoiachin was even given a royal seat of honor in Babylon. God's people thrived in the land of their captivity as a result of praying for the welfare of their captors and the government that ruled over them.

Proverbs 29:2 says, "When the righteous are in authority, the people rejoice; but when a wicked man rules, the people groan" (NKJV). It behooves us, therefore, to leverage every tool in our arsenal to support our leaders spiritually. That includes leaders on both sides of the aisle, regardless of which side you're on.

## Do Your Homework

Our robust participation in civic life is essential to sustaining our government as we know it. Without it, a government that is of the people, by the people, and for the people cannot endure. That's why our declining level of civic engagement is particularly troubling to me. Evidence of this reality is reflected in Americans' ignorance of civic fundamentals. Today, less than half of Americans can name all three branches of government, and only 24% know that freedom of religion is a First Amendment right.[7]

I'm not sure if Christians are more or less civically educated than the average non-Christian American. However, given the high turnout of mainstream evangelicals and those in the African American church, we're at least as much, if not more, inclined to vote. I just wonder how educated we are when we show up at the ballot box. The fact that there's such an extreme partisan split along racial and denominational lines makes me think that someone other than God is shaping our perspectives on the issues.

I urge everyone to do as much research on the issues and candidates as possible. As noted in the chapter titled "Wise as Serpents," we shouldn't just accept what politicians tell us they stand for. Rather, we should do our own homework to ensure that (a) we're focused on God's priorities, (b) the candidates are who they say they are, and (c) the policies that we ultimately support are just, wise, and the most likely to promote human flourishing.

## Get Out the Vote

Unlike most people in the world today, Americans have the unique privilege of influencing our own political destiny. God has given us stewardship over our government and expects us to manage it responsibly. For me, voting is a way of expressing my faith; I think of it as an intercessory prayer of sorts. By stepping up to vote, I'm standing in the gap for America and asking God to move in tangible ways.

Moreover, since the government has influence over everything that we do, we'd be fools *not* to vote. For though we are "sojourners and exiles" (1 Peter 2:11 ESV), God has positioned us here and now to be a blessing to America. Thus, we should vote in a way that advances the welfare of our country, even if it isn't our eternal home.

## Excuses, Excuses

No matter how convincing my arguments may be, some will still come up with excuses for not engaging politically. Every nasty Twitter exchange and negative campaign ad serves as ammunition for the voices in their heads screaming, "Get out, steer clear, and stay home!" But while many of our reactions are emotional, others are legitimate. Here are the ones I hear most often, which represent a mix of both.

**Politics are evil.** I recently read an article titled "12 Reasons Christians Should Not Be Involved in Politics."[8] A sampling of the list includes:

1. Politics are corrupt.
2. Politics divide us.
3. Jesus wasn't political.
4. God chooses our leaders (so what's the point in getting involved?).
5. We should focus on God's work (rather than the devil's—i.e., politics).

It's hard to argue directly with any of these points because factually, they're true. Politics *are* corrupt and divisive; Jesus *wasn't* overtly political; God *does* choose our leaders; and we should *always* focus on God's work above all else. But these arguments only tell one side of the story. Moreover, they fail to acknowledge that when we act in God's power, we can shift what politics currently *are* to what God intends them to *become*.

At the heart of this list lies the false belief that a sacred-secular divide exists, and that "God things" consist of only those done in the context of full-time vocational ministry. I grew up believing this lie, too, because I never met anyone at church who talked about doing things for God outside of it.

It wasn't until my early twenties that I realized that ministry isn't the only vocation through which God can work. Those working outside of the church in the marketplace, entertainment, education, and government are all in full-time ministry if their focus is on advancing the kingdom of God. The attitudes and intentions of people who work in "secular" jobs often fit the definition of "ministry" to a T. They include my best friend, who homeschools four children under the age of thirteen; my fellow attorneys who fight for godly principles of justice; CEOs who advance kingdom work through their companies; and government officials who promote laws and regulations that align with God's will for our nation.

It also dawned on me that Jesus himself was a carpenter, and that some of the most transformational Christians in history were not just ministers, but also politicians, teachers, entrepreneurs, parents, executives, mechanics, and musicians.

I now recognize that God can use anyone to bring His will into fruition. Consequently, I view everything I do, including politics, as full-time ministry. I've also realized that, like money and power, politics is neither good nor bad in and of itself. Rather, politics takes on the nature of those who wield it, for better or worse. When godly people flood politics with the intention of serving God, government is transformed from corrupt and divisive to just and unifying.

**Politics are a waste of my time.** Many Americans have been led to believe that "the whole system is rigged," either by people or God. Consequently, they wonder why they should waste their time engaging in politics at all. But imagine if we applied the same mentality to praying. Using the same logic, their question would be, what's the sense of praying if our lives are already predestined? Aren't we wasting time and energy thinking that anything we do or say can change God's mind?

The fact is, God always asks us to partner with Him to bring His will to pass. As Christ's co-laborers, Scripture tells us to "ask, seek, and knock," not once, but persistently, for that which we desire (Matthew 7:7–8). Asking and seeking are spiritual actions, which position us in a petitioning posture before God. But knocking is a physical action, which requires us to act. Asking God for His best for our country equates to praying for His will. Knocking equates to civic engagement, which is required to bring His will to pass.

So yes, God ultimately chooses our leaders—just as He ordains everything that happens in the world. But that doesn't preclude us from doing our part, just as trusting Him to provide doesn't preclude us from having to work. Moreover, a single prayer can bend God's ear, and even cause Him to change His mind. Moses proved the truth of this when God wanted to destroy the Israelites and his intercession caused God to spare them (Exodus 32:9–14). God is inclined to answer our prayers, especially when we do our part.

As for elections being rigged by humans—which we hear so much about these days—evidence of voter fraud has existed for decades. I witnessed this firsthand in Nevada while monitoring polling places in Washoe County. My job was to learn Nevada's election laws and look for any questionable activities happening in and around polling places. I didn't expect much of anything to happen, so what I saw shocked me. Nevada's election laws allow non-English speakers to ask anyone to help them vote. But those who'd positioned themselves to help were actually organized partisan operators. Since the definition of *help* wasn't clear in the context of Nevada's election laws, the "helpers" not only accompanied voters into the voting booths, but also picked up a stylus and voted for them!

As a poll-watching attorney whose sole purpose was to catch this type of fraud, I wrote down what I saw and took eyewitness statements from other onlookers. Then I submitted my reports to the Secretary of State. To my surprise, nothing was done with the information I provided. As elected officials, Secretaries of State have their own political interests to protect. And since my interest in a fair election contradicted this official's interests, nothing happened with the evidence I presented.

My response, however, was not to tuck my tail and concede defeat. My answer instead was to pursue justice by helping to elect better Secretaries of State. They are the guardians of our votes, so it's critical that impartial people of the highest integrity are elected to fill their positions. I do my best to educate myself and others as to why we need to pay attention to lower-profile offices like these, which we might otherwise overlook to our nation's detriment.

One other point I cannot overstate is that *every vote matters*. In the 2000 presidential election, President George W. Bush won Florida by a mere 537 votes. In the same election, he lost the state of New Mexico by just 366 votes. Given all that happened in President Bush's first term, I'll bet many people would have prioritized voting differently if they could turn back time. Since we never know what's coming down the pike, the best action we can take is to vote. We may not know everything there is to know about the candidates, but with God's help, we can make the best decisions with the information we have.

**I have no idea where to even start.** For those who *do* want to get involved, politics can seem overwhelming. I certainly felt that way in college until I read a book my professor wrote called "Just Do It!" It urged its readers to dive into politics by simply getting involved. I took his advice literally, which is how my career in politics began.

Getting involved was harder for my mom, who didn't speak much English when she first moved to America. With a limited understanding of electoral politics, she sat on the sidelines until she met and married my dad. I'm proud to say that voter education initiatives have changed that for many immigrants today. But if you find yourself feeling like my mom did, I urge you to ask someone who's involved in politics to let you tag along. I guarantee you'll find someone who'll be happy to teach you everything you need to know.

I am proud of the fact that my congressional campaign welcomed and offered hands-on training to political neophytes of all backgrounds. From elementary schoolers to college students, new immigrants to full-fledged citizens, homemakers to CEOs, and everyone in between, our headquarters buzzed with the thrill of democracy. As an American, I consider it my personal responsibility to not only welcome but invite people into our democratic processes with wide-open arms. Being able to do that on my own campaign was a dream come true—and something that made my mom very proud of me as well.

## Diving In

When people tell us they're getting involved in politics, we often assume that means they're running for office. While that might be true for a handful of us, most get involved in equally important, but less time-consuming ways.

I volunteered on my first real campaign in college, helping my best friend's father educate voters on his "slow growth" initiative at shopping centers. I didn't know much about the issue other than that he was trying to protect the farmland surrounding our home from being overtaken by developers. My father, a capitalist to the core, was firmly against everything I advocated for. But as a nineteen-year-old, I felt great standing for something—anything, really—and urging others to do the same.

That campaign piqued my interest in studying government in college, where I was mentored by a brilliant political strategist, Professor Christian Potholm. "Prof P" had also started his political career at Bowdoin, where he helped prepare his roommate, William Cohen, for public office. "Billy," as my professor called him, successfully ran for Bangor City Council, Mayor, Maine's Second Congressional District, and one of Maine's two Senate seats before being appointed Secretary of Defense by President Bill Clinton. With Prof P as his political advisor, he was unstoppable.

When I decided to work in politics, Prof P sent my résumé to two campaigns: Elizabeth "Liddy" Dole's and George W.

Bush's. Weeks later, my father and I drove to Austin, Texas, to launch my career as an intern on Governor Bush's campaign. I was relieved it worked out the way it did since Liddy Dole ended up dropping out of the primary. Working on Governor Bush's campaign led to a career in Washington, DC, where I worked in the White House, the US Department of Justice, and the US Senate.

After graduating from law school in 2007, I joined a large international law firm. There, I was able to turn my political contacts and legal education into a paycheck—and a fun one at that. Through my firm, I maintained my political involvement, attending the 2008 Republican National Convention and volunteering to monitor polls as a member of the Republican National Lawyers Association. Meanwhile, with every election cycle, my desire to run for federal office intensified.

As a Republican living in overwhelmingly Democratic DC (by a 9 to 1 ratio), I knew I had to leave Washington to find a winnable district. So I moved to my favorite city, San Diego, where Republicans still won elections, and I could live the life I'd always dreamt of.

After spending four years in San Diego and volunteering for other campaigns, I decided to go all in myself. It seemed like the perfect cycle to run. Republicans were expected to win big in 2016, and I wanted to capitalize on the incoming red wave. So I threw my hat in the race for California's Fifty-second Congressional District, finally fulfilling my ambition. While I didn't win the general election that year, running was, on balance, one of the most gratifying things I've ever done in my life. Speaking passionately about issues I cared about, for a cause greater than myself, made me come alive.

Today, I'm just as involved as ever, though more so behind the scenes. I host fundraisers, contribute, and campaign for candidates and causes I believe in. I advise aspiring politicians on the dos and don'ts of campaigning and encourage young

leaders to get involved early. In my work as a public affairs consultant, I have the privilege of advocating for policies I believe
in, and I love what I get paid to do in the halls of Capitol Hill.

Over time, I've come to realize that *everything* we do that
touches the political realm matters. As a nineteen-year-old
talking to folks in shopping centers, I spoke words that made
people think about what they wanted their city to look like.
As a twenty-two-year-old campaigning for George W. Bush, I
helped Latinos realize they'd have a voice and a champion in
the White House. As a staffer in the Bush administration, I supported those who navigated uncharted territory in our Global
War on Terrorism. As a Senate law clerk, I helped confirm the
Chief Justice of the Supreme Court of the United States. And
as a congressional candidate, I engaged constituents on all ends
of the political spectrum, welcoming their participation in our
democratic process. In every political activity I've participated
in, my goal was to leave my country better off than I found it.
And working toward that goal, regardless of the outcomes,
gives me a great deal of satisfaction.

My point is, there are myriad ways to get involved in shaping
our nation's political future. You don't have to be a campaign
junkie, move to Washington, DC, or run for office like me. You
can actually do a lot from the comfort of your hometown, such
as be a poll worker, contribute money to a candidate or cause,
host a town hall, invite a politician to speak at an event, march
for a cause, register new voters, volunteer for a campaign, or
work for an elected official. Whatever God puts on your heart to
change or support, He provides a way for you to follow through
on. Ask Him what He wants you to focus on and how to get
involved. And be ready to walk through doors that will seemingly magically open to you.

Generally, we tend to hate what we have not experienced or
do not understand. In America, politics are easily accessible
to everyone—there's no barrier to entry or reason to stand on

the sidelines. So rather than hating politics, try embracing it instead. Considering how great a blessing and awesome a responsibility we bear, it's worth diving in.

## REFLECTION

1. What's *really* holding you back from getting involved in politics? Is it apathy, fear, misunderstanding, or disgust? If so, where does the feeling originate from, and what does God say about it?
2. What issues or candidates matter most to you in the upcoming election cycle?
3. What can you do with the time and resources you have to effect political change?

## PRAYER

*Thank you, Lord, for the freedom we have to love and worship you in America. Make me a good steward of the blessings and opportunities you've given me to bring godly principles into the political arena. Rid me of any false and limiting beliefs that keep me from getting involved. Use my participation to glorify you and bless our nation. In Jesus' name, Amen.*

# THE THIRD OPTION

There is a battle going on in the natural world, and the devil is trying to get you to take sides. Make sure that your side is Jesus' side, and that you're praying for all involved.

—Pastor Miles McPherson

In 2017, Pastor Miles McPherson, founder and senior pastor of the Rock Church in San Diego, sent me a draft of his book on racial reconciliation. He asked me to critique it from a politically conservative perspective. In it, I read both heartbreaking and encouraging stories of the many lessons he'd learned in his 60-plus years of living in America as a black man of mixed ethnicity (Jamaican, Caucasian, and a pinch of Asian). Before reading it, I'd been a little starstruck by my pastor; after all, he was a former NFL player for the San Diego Chargers, and he'd founded and led one of the largest and most ethnically diverse churches in America. Everything about his biography indicated that he'd lived a charmed life. Reading his story, however, gave me a very different perspective on his formative years and helped me appreciate the challenges he had to overcome in order to survive and succeed.

As a half-Chinese, half-Caucasian woman who's had no experience with the type of racism he's encountered, I didn't think I had much to contribute to his book. Sure, I'm a minority, but I'm one that blends in relatively easily with "mainstream" Americans. As such, I didn't really feel qualified to comment on his perspectives. But after diving into his book, I realized that its underlying theme was God's desire to unify His people, a message that I certainly ascribe to and yearn to see manifested myself. Given that race, socioeconomics, religion, and politics are among the top fault lines along which our nation tends to fracture, my experience working in politics gave me plenty of insight to add. We ended up working together for the next six months, perfecting his message and striking a balance of hard-hitting truths and grace-filled lessons on how to love our racially diverse neighbors.

## God's Side

The title Pastor Miles settled on for his book was *The Third Option*. This title fits the book's message perfectly. It speaks to the two options culture tells us to choose between—*our* side or *theirs*—versus the third option God asks us to pick: *His*. A similar choice was presented to Joshua as he led the Israelites into the Promised Land.

Joshua was readying himself for the battle of Jericho when he looked up and saw a man standing in front of him with a drawn sword in his hand. Ready to rumble, Joshua approached the stranger and asked, "Are you for us or for our enemies?" (Joshua 5:13). Given the circumstances, Joshua needed to know—after all there could only be two answers, right? So imagine Joshua's surprise when the man replied, "Neither, but as commander of the army of the Lord I have now come" (Joshua 5:14).

His answer elicited an appropriate response from Joshua, who fell face down in reverence before the man. "What message does my Lord have for his servant?" he asked with what I can only imagine was a trembling voice and submissive spirit (Joshua 5:14). Any prior concerns about who was on whose side evaporated in light of the overarching significance of the one who stood before him.

In the context of politics, Christians are faced with a similar choice as to whom they will side with. Most of us think that our options are limited to picking between two political parties. But I believe God would have us choose a third option that transcends our party affiliation: His side, His truth, and His ways.

Joshua made his once-and-for-all choice early in life: to follow the Lord first and only. His wholehearted commitment to God is what qualified him to lead the Israelites into the Promised Land. The Israelites, however, wavered in their commitment to God, choosing instead to flirt with the idols of those in the lands they conquered. Turning their backs on God, they looked to foreign cultures for guidance in how to think, live, and worship. Their wishy-washiness incensed Joshua, prompting him to tell them to "choose this day whom you will serve"— the living God of Israel, or something less (Joshua 24:15 ESV).

God is asking Americans the same question today. As Christians living in a land of freedom and abundance, we are blessed beyond measure. He has given us everything, including the choice of whether we'll follow Him or not. And, like the Israelites, we're prone to choosing lesser gods—especially when it comes to politics. Charismatic leaders, impassioned movements, and our own emotions have a way of diverting our affections from God. Moreover, politics causes us to point our fingers at other people, while Joshua's question is leveled squarely at *us*: whom or what are *we* serving—the Lord or a political agenda? Joshua's answer was unequivocal, and ours should be as well: "As for me and my house, we will serve the Lord" (Joshua 24:15 ESV).

## Unequivocal Truth and Honor

It's admittedly challenging to understand what "choosing God" means in politics. After all, our choices in the ballot box are generally limited to one of two parties. Would choosing God potentially mean giving up on politics entirely?

The answer to that question is a clear and direct no. God does not expect His children to withdraw from our political system or render themselves irrelevant by setting up camp on the fringes of society. Rather, He wants us to work through the systems we currently live in and influence them from within. In the same way that Joshua continued fighting for Israel as it conquered occupied lands, we, too, should continue fighting for godly principles in a manner that reflects our loyalty to Him. It doesn't really matter which party we sign up to support. What matters is that we always choose God by standing on His unequivocal truth.

Jesus modeled this way of living for us by working through human institutions of religion and government. He didn't show up on earth and blow the temple to smithereens or overthrow politicians He didn't like. In fact, He not only engaged humanity through them, but He also respected their authority. His loyalty, however, wasn't to their doctrines or ways of doing things. His loyalty was to God alone, however high the cost.

As His disciples, we are faced with the same choices that Jesus had to make. Like Jesus, we should respect human authorities and governmental institutions. But our loyalty should be to God above our earthly affiliations, a choice that may be costly, but well worth the price. Choosing God over political conformity empowers us to facilitate supernatural outcomes.

And supernatural outcomes are what our nation needs more than anything right now.

## Discerning God's Truth

There's plenty to debate in terms of *how* we choose to implement God's truths. But *what* the truth actually *is,* is clearly addressed in Scripture. Unlike many of our politicians, God isn't subject to "fuzzy math" or "misstatements of fact." As the psalmist says, "The entirety of [God's Word] is truth" (Psalm 119:160 NKJV). Therefore, we may argue over *which* of God's truths to emphasize, and *how* our politicians should implement them. But *what* God stands for and against is clearly expressed—whether in Scripture, through divine revelation, or by nature itself.

Psalm 19 vividly expresses God's desire to make His truth known: "The heavens declare the glory of God; the skies proclaim the work of his hands. Day after day they pour forth speech; night after night they reveal knowledge" (Psalm 19:1–2). In other parts of Scripture, God uses a donkey (Numbers 22:28), a burning bush (Exodus 3:2), and a gentle breeze (1 Kings 19:12) to express His truths to mankind. Jesus even told the Pharisees that if the multitudes praising Him were silenced, the stones would cry out in their place (Luke 19:40). God is eager to share His eternal truths with us—and He'll do whatever it takes to get His point across.

Nevertheless, many are apt to ignore Him when they hear a hard truth that is difficult to accept. This is especially true of people like me, who enjoy winning popularity contests. There are truths in the Bible that some of us would rather modify, temper, or ignore. But love cannot exist—in politics, policies, or politicians—apart from God's truth. As Father Joe Campbell writes, "There is a deeply profound connection between love and truth: you cannot have one without the other. If you ignore the truth . . . you may not only fail to love in that situation. You may even wind up causing great harm."[1] Choosing God, therefore, means choosing to represent His truth regardless of the consequences.

## Honoring Others

In addition to choosing His truth, siding with God requires us to honor one another. Romans 12:10 tells us to go above and beyond by "honor[ing] one another above ourselves." As easy as this sounds in theory, this is especially hard to put into practice in politics. Let's face it—people are annoying, especially when they think that *they're* always right and *you're* always wrong. But regardless of how annoying others might be, God still commands us to treat them honorably.

You might wonder why God is so intent on our honoring one another when some seem undeserving of it. He answers that question in the first book of the Bible by establishing that all people are made in His likeness (Genesis 1:26–27). Jesus added even greater value to our lives when He laid His down for ours. Our value is therefore inherent and unequivocal—based not on what others think of us, or what we think of ourselves, but rather whose image we reflect and the sacrifice Jesus made on our behalf. No political opinion or party affiliation can add to or diminish our worth.

The Declaration of Independence affirms our value by expressing that which is "self-evident": that "all men are created equal," and that "they are endowed by their Creator with certain unalienable Rights."[2] Unalienable means "not capable of being taken away or denied."[3] Thus, our founding documents underscore the fact that nothing can diminish anyone's inherent value and worth. So if we're truly committed to choosing the third option, then we must honor people the way God calls us to, no matter what they stand for, buy into, or believe.

## Redefining In-Groups

Social scientists have discovered that one way divisive mentalities emerge is through our tendency to apply in-group bias—that is, preferential treatment—to those who constitute our in-group, or those who are "like us." This is something that literally everyone is guilty of—not intentionally, but because we are socially conditioned this way. We're all more comfortable with those who are like us, a fact that we must accept in order to overcome.

In-grouping threatens our unity, as Pastor Miles explains in his book:

> Any group in power favors its own in the media, in legal systems, in the corporate world, and whenever opportunities arise to reinforce their own positions of power. . . . False stereotypes about the less favored groups develop, and are reinforced through the [in-group's] narratives. This self-perpetuating system can strengthen the prevailing power structure of a city, state, or nation for generations.[4]

The reason that in- and out-grouping threatens our unity is that nobody is okay with being an "out-grouper" forever. At some point, people will stop accepting their marginalization and stand up for themselves—often in ways that pit in- and out-groups more firmly against each other. Sometimes, we're able to overcome these issues together, through education and civil discourse. When we can't, violence ensues, shaking the very foundations of our nation.

What matters, then, is how self-aware we are of how we treat those we disagree with. For some, speaking contemptuously about those in our "out-group" is celebrated as the norm. If you're wondering if that's you, reflect on how you refer to those whose politics differ from yours. Do you consider them ignorant, evil, subhuman, or worse? If so, how do your thoughts manifest in your treatment of them?

World-renowned relationship expert Dr. John Gottman is famous for identifying "The Four Horsemen of the Apocalypse" in regard to relationships. In his forty years of research, Gottman has identified the four most destructive relational behaviors: criticism, contempt, defensiveness, and stonewalling—the worst of these being contempt.[5] Contempt is manifested in myriad ways: verbally through the expression of hostile humor, sarcasm, mockery, name-calling, and mimicking, as well as nasty things we write about others on social media; and non-verbally through offensive body language such as eye-rolling and sneering. All of these behaviors are accepted as "politics as usual." And all express our contempt for those Jesus commanded us to love.

We must, therefore, change the way we think about our neighbors and political enemies so that we stop treating them with contempt. The only way to do that is by redefining our in-group bias to include those we formerly regarded as members of our out-group. Doing so is *not* easy, given how regularly politics reinforces our desire to pick a side. However, by redefining who our in-group entails—that is, changing our language and thoughts about our political enemies so that we start viewing them as family, coworkers, and friends—we can "be transformed by the renewing of our minds" (Romans 12:2) and reject culture's efforts to divide us.

## Eliminate Blind Spots

Another great point my pastor makes in his book is that no matter how Christlike we are, we all have blind spots. A blind spot, by definition, is something we can't see. It's not a matter of not wanting to; it's a matter of not being able to. It's normal to have blind spots in different aspects of our lives, and just as blind spots exist from the driver's seat of our cars, blind spots exist for us in the political realm as well.

Our political blind spots stem from what a group of Princeton researchers refer to as "our inability to recognize the impact of our biases and limitations on our judgment, behavior and decisions."[6] We assume our biases are trustworthy and that we are immune to them. Our psychological biases deceive us by labeling *others* as biased, while tricking us into believing that *we* are impartial and objective. Such denial weakens our ability to discern truth, making it harder for us to remain humble and self-aware. Thus, blind spots also make it difficult to appreciate political perspectives that challenge our own.

The good news is that, just as in driving, a turn of the head and a new vantage point can quickly eliminate many of our blind spots. This obviously requires a desire to see things differently and a certain proactivity on our part; merely wishing our blind spots away is impossible without identifying them first. A good initial step, then, is to ask others—especially those who sit across the aisle—what we might be missing in our understanding of their perspectives. By listening and asking follow-up questions, we can all become more enlightened, educated, and empathetic, making it easier to recognize our blind spots for what they really are.

## Walk a Mile

One of the many things I love about my pastor is that he never challenges anyone to do something that he isn't willing to do himself. One of the challenges he poses, especially to White congregants in his church, is to take a "field trip" and "walk a mile" in the shoes of minorities: entering their neighborhoods, going to their barbershops, eating in their restaurants, and experiencing what it's like to be a minority for a day. This experience is so daunting that many chicken out at the last minute, even after accepting his challenge. But those who follow through find that their understanding of minority mindsets and experiences is utterly transformed, as is their inclination to love and honor those they may have formerly categorized as "others."

This challenge is completely perspective-shifting. It literally puts people in the midst of those they do not understand and forces them to reexamine their long-held beliefs in light of others' realities. It is an invaluable learning experience if we're willing to undertake it, but it can also be quite painful.

My only experience of feeling like a "minority" was attending Georgetown University Law Center as an evening student. I worked with Republicans by day and attended law school with mostly Democrats at night.

In my first year of law school, I worked for Attorney General John Ashcroft at the US Department of Justice as a member of the Bush administration. At the time, my job was to traipse around the country and convince state and local governments of the necessity of reauthorizing the Patriot Act. It was a thankless job that people on both sides of the aisle hated me for.

After a long day's work, I'd drag myself to class at 5:30 p.m. for four hours of intense learning. The majority of my professors were Democrats who'd worked in Democratic administrations or for Democratic members of Congress. This was true of many of my classmates as well. Meanwhile, most of my work colleagues were dyed-in-the-wool conservatives who shared my political convictions. Consequently, I clashed with my professors and fellow students on a regular basis, but never more than late one Friday evening as we wrapped up a Constitutional law class.

On that fateful evening, I asked a question that I knew might be taken out of context, but it was one that I needed to know the answer to. Even so, I regretted asking it the moment it escaped my mouth. My professor, a former Clinton appointee, turned around, pointed a finger at me, and yelled, "*YOU* are what's wrong with democracy! It's people like you and your president who make a mockery of our Constitution!" Meanwhile, a few of my classmates chimed in on her side, calling me a fascist and other unflattering names. I was aghast—I'd worked my tail off traveling all around the country, trying to protect America from the next 9/11, and all I got was grief in return. I'd never felt so misunderstood and mischaracterized, but it dawned on me while driving home that many of my Democratic friends must feel the same way when Republicans unfairly labeled them as socialists, communists, or worse.

That experience taught me a painful but necessary lesson: we can't possibly know what other people are thinking, feeling, or motivated by, no matter what they say or do. We might *think* we know, but our blind spots will always ascribe the best of intentions to ourselves, and the worst of intentions to those we consider our enemies. That doesn't make us bad people— only human—but we do have a responsibility to rise above our natural instincts. The Holy Spirit empowers us to transcend our human reactions by enabling us to supernaturally love those we appear to have little in common with. The irony is that, when we do, we realize that we're more alike than we are different.

## Honorable Assumptions

The last point I'll extract from my pastor's book is that honoring people means making honorable assumptions about them. Scripture tells us that "God does not see as man sees, since man looks at the outward appearance, but the Lord looks at the heart" (1 Samuel 16:7 NASB). This is as much a statement of fact as it is an admonition for us to be more God-like in our perspectives. It also explains why we should avoid ascribing motives to others when we're not God and cannot see into other people's hearts.

We all have feelings that we harbor toward others, both good and bad. The good obviously accompanies those we "get"— people we agree with and who affirm us, including those who share our political convictions. Those we don't "get"—whose experiences we haven't shared and that we don't understand—are far likelier to face our questioning, criticism, and scrutiny.

The most honoring way to engage those we disagree with is by making honorable assumptions about them from the get-go. Rather than ascribing ill intentions or assigning made-up beliefs, we should ask honest questions that get to the heart of their interests and concerns. There's always more to one's political opinions than meets the naked eye, and it behooves us to find out what that is for others, as well as ourselves. Whether or not it changes our opinions, it will help us foster unity.

I put these principles into regular use in one of my closest friendships. Andrea's politics run as counter to mine as anyone's ever could—and yet, over the years, we've nurtured a friendship that has withstood both Obama's and Trump's presidencies, as well as the overturning of *Roe v. Wade*. A central tenet of our friendship is our commitment to make honorable assumptions of each other whenever we don't understand what the other is saying. We don't ask "gotcha" questions or put a political spin on our answers because what we *really* want is to *understand* each other. Even when we cannot agree on facts and premises, we've learned to respect one another's opinions. At times that comes with tears and hurt feelings, but since we're firmly committed to our friendship, it never derails us for long. Our friendship grows stronger and stronger over time because we feel safe being honest with each other. It's freeing to know that we can be ourselves, regardless of our difference in opinions.

Jesus modeled this principle beautifully throughout His ministry. When people were angry and accusatory, He addressed their underlying spiritual and emotional needs rather than responding to them in kind. Take, for example, the story of Lazarus's death and resurrection. Lazarus was one of Jesus' closest friends, so when Lazarus fell ill, his sisters sent a message to Jesus that said, "Lord, the one you love is sick" (John

11:3). However, when Jesus heard the news, He waited a few more days before going to Lazarus's hometown of Bethany.

When Jesus finally arrived, Lazarus had already been dead for four days. When Martha discovered that Jesus was close, she went out to meet Him and give Him a piece of her mind. "Lord," she said, angrily and accusatorily I'd imagine, "if you had been here, my brother would not have died." Jesus felt the weight of her emotions and recognized that she was grieving over her brother's death. Rather than rebuke Martha for speaking to Him in such a manner, Jesus joined her in weeping (John 11:35). Jesus chose to experience her pain rather than respond to Martha in anger.

We all know what happened next—Jesus performed a miracle and raised Lazarus from the grave. This story offers us an amazing example of God's remarkable power to resurrect. But an even greater lesson for real-life application is how Jesus responded to His friends: sharing their grief and addressing their needs rather than responding to their anger.

My therapist once told me that when people act angrily, we're only seeing the tip of their iceberg. He said that a mere 10% of an iceberg can be seen above water, while 90% is submerged below the surface. Underneath anger lies hurt; beneath that, fear; and at its base, unmet needs. So when people respond to us with anger, he said, we should put our reactions on pause and try to discover what lies below the surface. If we can address their underlying emotional needs rather than confront their anger head on, we can help alleviate their fears and acknowledge the source of their pain.

Imagine how revolutionary it would be if we applied this psychological principle to politics! It would literally change everything about how we respond to those we disagree with. By honoring who they are and how they feel, we can point them to the One who can meet all of their needs. Thus, choosing the third option transforms politics into a conduit of God's love for humanity.

## REFLECTION

1. Do you choose the third option consistently as it pertains to your political positions?
2. How well do you honor those you disagree with?
3. Who can you practice addressing 90% of the iceberg with, so that you can become a more compassionate and loving reflection of Jesus?

## PRAYER

*Lord, I've allowed myself to be more influenced by politics than by your holy truths. My blind spots are significant, and I want to be rid of them once and for all. Correct me when I make assumptions about others that are anything less than honorable. Teach me how to meet people in the place of their greatest need, so that I can respond rather than react to their pain. Use me, Lord, to be a conduit of your love through my political engagement. In Jesus' name, Amen.*

## 15

# UNITED WE STAND

*In essentials, unity. In nonessentials, liberty. In all things, love.*
— Marco Antonio de Dominis

In 2001, I led a prayer group with now-Congressman (then-White House staffer) Jodey Arrington. I barely remember how we started it or why, but an email he recently forwarded to me from way back then gave me insight into our intentions. In it was my response to a question he asked about the structure of our group: "Yes to a general structure of worship, reflection, and prayer, but with great flexibility to let the Spirit lead and direct." In other words, I didn't see this as being "our group," but rather God's, to lead.

We launched this group, comprised of people from all walks of life, without knowing what it would ultimately be. And the people we attracted were absolutely remarkable. There were those, like us, who served in the White House, civil servants from various federal agencies, businesspeople, ministry leaders, and men and women experiencing homelessness. Under no circumstances would anyone looking at us from the outside think that we had anything in common—after all, Jodey and I lived in suits, while our homeless brothers and sisters rode in on wheelchairs or limped in shoeless to take their rightful spot in our circle. And our differences didn't stop there, either— those who worshiped with us represented every denomination imaginable, from AME to Baptist to Methodist to Catholic. What leveled the playing field, despite our denominational differences, was our equality at the foot of the cross.

I share this story wistfully because it's hard to imagine a group like this worshiping together today. This all happened over twenty years ago, when politics, race, and socioeconomics were less overtly divisive than they are now. Back then, nothing could keep us from worshiping Jesus as a family. If we tried to bring a group like this together today, Jodey, being the leader he is in Congress, wouldn't be able to share his heart freely without fear of a video leak. Nor would White House staffers, given the presence of those on the other side of the aisle. I even wonder if our Black brothers and sisters would feel comfortable hanging out with a bunch of buttoned-up White people, given the racial division in America today. Would we all feel too committed to our cultural, racial, and political loyalties to gather together as the body of Christ?

I'm afraid the answer is yes, given how readily we self-segregate. What saddens me most is that the same division in culture has crept into the church itself. Sunday mornings have always been the most racially segregated time of the week in America.[1] I had no awareness of this reality before I read it, since my pastor jokes that ours is a "Skittles" church, where people of every color, race, and background worship together. But apparently, most Christians in America choose to attend churches with people who look, talk, and think just like them. They also choose churches that align with their political affiliations. This reality emboldens some pastors to openly endorse candidates from the pulpit, an act that not only jeopardizes their nonprofit tax status, but also distracts from the reason we're there in the first place: to learn about the only One who can save our nation and our souls.

Nevertheless, the church is split along the same red and blue lines as culture is today—possibly even more so, since activism from each party's base is rooted in the church. Recent polls show that upwards of 80% of congregants in certain denominations belong to the same political party.[2] This explains how some Christians grow so extreme in their beliefs. It's nearly impossible *not* to conform when everyone around you asserts that the only godly way of thinking is theirs. Which is fine; the point of this book isn't to convince people to neutralize or drop their convictions. Rather, the point is that our convictions should never be allowed to override God's exhortation to unify.

## The Overriding Importance of Unity

I started this book with a chapter titled "Indivisible," and I'm ending it with a chapter titled "United We Stand." The bookending of this topic is intentional; unity is both my opening statement and closing argument. Since we can no longer look to churches as models of unity, we must commit to taking on the cause ourselves. And it's a cause that rightly belongs to us, because of all people, Christians understand the importance of unity best.

It's impossible to read the Bible without stumbling across a teaching on unity; after all, there are 179 verses that speak to it. I listed many of them in the opening chapter, and it's worth reiterating some of them here:

I appeal to you, brothers and sisters, in the name of our Lord Jesus Christ, that all of you agree with one another in what you say and that there be no divisions among you, but that you be perfectly united in mind and thought.

> 1 Corinthians 1:10

I in them and you in me—so that they may be brought to complete unity. Then the world will know that you sent me and have loved them even as you have loved me.

> John 17:23

He is the embodiment of our peace, sent once and for all to take down the great barrier of hatred and hostility that has divided us so that we can be one.

> Ephesians 2:14 VOICE

And my personal favorite:

There is neither Jew nor Gentile, neither slave nor free, nor is there male and female, [nor Republican or Democrat], for you are all one in Christ Jesus.

> Galatians 3:28, Denise Standard Version

As these verses make clear, you can't call yourself a serious Christian and not take God's teaching on unity seriously.

One of the blessings that stems from unity is greater authority in the political sphere. Sure, it might cost us our pride, and require us to hang up our boxing gloves, but by trading both for love, we're better able to influence others. Imagine how a unified church would look to a watching world, witnessing the full body of Christ—not just those sharing our pews—share the political burdens that their brothers and sisters across the aisle carry. Even if we disagree as to how we'd address those burdens, acknowledging them as important to a member of our spiritual family would set an unprecedented example of unity. By rising above the political fray, Christians would become the most powerful constituency in America. As Martin Luther King Jr. noted, "Love is the only force capable of transforming an enemy into a friend."[3] Since we need a lot of friends to effect political change, loving unity is a wise and essential start.

Pursuing unity is not—as many characterize it—liberal, fluffy, or soft. Neither is it optional. And unity is certainly not the same thing as conformity. Just because we've been reconciled to each other by the cross doesn't mean that our differences magically disappear. In fact, we are called to unify *in spite of* our differences. Our pursuit of unity stems from our common identity as brothers and sisters in Christ. Unity is therefore our response to God's command, fueled by our love for each other and our desire to obey Him.

Conformity, on the other hand, stems from external pressures that tell us to be or believe something for the sake of getting along with others. Conformity stems from religious and political spirits demanding that we adhere to human standards rather than God's. Fueled by the fear of people, conformity drives us to extremes and threatens our ability to love and honor each other the way God commands us to.

Political extremism is anathema to unity and should thus be avoided by Christians. It breeds hatred and suspicion and fuels the "us versus them" mentality that Satan uses to "steal, kill, and destroy" (John 10:10) the church. It also causes us to demonize half of the population in America based on their party affiliation, which makes it harder to see them as made in the image of God.

As Christians, we should direct our hatred at that which divides us rather than at those who don't vote like we do. If we're praying for a heart after God's—one that loves what He loves and hates what He hates—people and division must be at the top of each list. As Scripture says, we do not wrestle against flesh and blood, but rather the principalities of darkness (Ephesians 6:12). Satan's only aim is to divide and conquer. Division itself is thus our common enemy, and overcoming it is every Christian's responsibility.

## Priorities

When asked what God prioritizes for us, most Christians respond correctly: loving God and our neighbors, including our enemies (Matthew 22:37–40). It would make sense, then, that we'd rearrange our actions, thoughts, and prayers accordingly. Rather than wake up and turn on the news, we might decide, instead, to take a moment to say good morning to our neighbors, make breakfast for our family, or read Scripture. There's nothing inherently wrong with watching the news in the morning; it just shouldn't take priority over other actions we can take to love God and people. By acting lovingly toward others, we fulfill Jesus' commandment to "do good," even to those who hate us (Luke 6:27).

Disciplining our thoughts is another area in which priorities matter. Rather than let negative, hateful thoughts of others take up any of our mental real estate, we should condition our minds to view people the way God does: as precious and beloved. Whatever they've said or done to offend us we must take to the Lord and ask Him to deal with in our hearts. Our only job is to love them—not to avenge their offense. Imagine how powerful Christians could be if rather than cursing those we disagreed with (e.g., our least favorite politicians), we called out the gold in them instead? It might take some digging to find that which God values in them, but it's in there somewhere, and God wants us to discover it.

Praying for our enemies is another way to love them well (Luke 6:28). I practiced doing this with my political opponent during my congressional race, and it really helped change my thoughts and actions toward him. Rather than pray solely for victory, I asked God to bless him and to encounter him personally. As the Reverend Billy Graham said, "You cannot pray for someone and hate them at the same time. Even if you are asking God to restrain their evil actions, you should also be praying that He will change their hearts."[4] If we all followed the reverend's advice, loving our enemies would be a whole lot easier.

## Pursuing Unity

Pursuing unity sounds fine and dandy until you try putting it into practice. As with love, unity is easier said than done. That's because dealing with people is always a challenge, whether you're in ministry, the marketplace, or in politics. Here are some practical tips that have helped me pursue unity, in politics and in other areas of my life.

**Pray for a desire to unify.** Uniting with those we agree with comes naturally, but uniting with those we have less in common with is hard. That's why it's so important that we ask God for the *desire* to unify. When the going gets tough, *wanting* to unify keeps us engaged and committed. One way I do this is by praying, "God, help me to love what you love and hate what you hate." This helps me separate people from their actions and aligns my desires with God's.

I highly recommend recruiting others to pray for unity with you. Praying together keeps us accountable and encourages us to prevail. In the same way churches counsel couples to pray for unity in their marriages, we should also encourage believers to pray for unity in America. As Scripture says, "two are better than one," and "a chord of three strands is not quickly broken" (Ecclesiastes 4:9–12). Make unity a theme with those you do life with, and every one of your relationships will change for the better.

**Make unity *your* priority.** When it comes to pursuing unity, practicing it in our daily lives is essential to seeing it come to pass. As Nelson Mandela said, "Until I changed myself I could not change others."[5] He's right; moving toward unity starts with a single individual's decision to initiate it.

We make decisions every day to either reject or embrace those we disagree with. Opportunities to do so sometimes come to us, whether in watercooler conversations with our coworkers or over Thanksgiving dinner with family. But sometimes, it takes initiative on our part, especially when we're surrounded by like-minded people. We should commit to doing things that put us outside our comfort zone. As suggested in the "walk a mile" exercise described in the previous chapter, getting immersive experience in another's life is a surefire way to increase empathy and understanding. A gesture as simple as asking someone who doesn't share your political beliefs to meet you for a walk or grab a cup of coffee is all it usually takes. Embarking on a new friendship, or holding on to an old one, is a great way to forge unity with those we disagree with politically.

**Do what's moral, not what's modeled.** This tip comes straight from Pastor Andy Stanley, and it's a good one. In a sermon delivered on Independence Day, Pastor Andy urged his congregation to do unto others, not as they do unto us, but as Jesus has done for us.[6] Culture leaves out the Jesus part but says essentially the same thing in the "Platinum Rule:" Treat others the way that *they* would like to be treated.

Whether we go with Pastor Andy's version or culture's, the point is the same: we should always do the loving thing, regardless of what anyone and everyone else is doing around us. This is a much-needed lesson now, when popular leaders have singlehandedly changed the political tenor of our nation and turned us against each other. The names I've called those I've disagreed with in the past are appalling and inconsistent with my faith. Like so many others, I've fallen in line with culture rather than leading people in a better direction.

In youth group, we were taught that Christians ought to be "thermostats, not thermometers." Thermostats set temperatures; thermometers merely reflect them. The Holy Spirit enables us to be thermostats, but the choice is still ours to make. If we choose to elevate how we treat one another, we can transform any room, platform, or environment we step into.

**Go first.** Leaders don't wait for others to act; they charge directly into dicey situations while everyone else stands on the sidelines. Leaders always go first, even when they stand alone.

Christians are called to lead. In their book *Designed to Lead*, authors Eric Geiger and Kevin Peck write that the church "is uniquely set apart to develop and deploy leaders for the glory of God and the advancement of the gospel."[7] They also quote Robert Quinn, who said that "leadership means go forth to die."[8] Dying to ourselves is the only way Jesus' life can be revealed within us (Galatians 2:20–21; 1 Corinthians 15:31). It's also the example Jesus set for us in laying His life down for ours (Mark 10:45).

Geiger and Peck remind us that leadership failures are often rooted in passivity. Sins of omission grieve God's heart as much as sins of commission. They use Adam to make this point, writing, "The failure of Adam's leadership in the garden was passivity, not aggression. Adam failed to cultivate the garden. Adam failed to keep the weeds out. [So] the weed of evil crawled into the garden in the form of a serpent,"[9] changing humanity's relationship with God forever.

As leaders we must not only initiate unity, but also cultivate our nation in such a way that we keep the weeds of division out. That can look like speaking truth to put a stop to the political spin cycle, refusing to denigrate politicians on the other side of the aisle, or initiating respectful conversations about your differences with others. There are myriad ways to go first, but if you can't think of one, ask God to help. And be prepared, because when you do, you'll be flooded with opportunities to lead.

**Back away from the line.** Growing up, I was inundated with a long list of to-dos that shaped my relationship with God.

This translated into the following belief system: if I *did* right, God would bless me, but if I *didn't*, I'd be cursed. Identifying the line that separated right from wrong became a full-time obsession. My goal, especially in my teens and twenties, was to see *how close* I could get to the line without stepping over it.

In the same way, laws draw lines between what's legal and what isn't, while our Constitution tells us our rights as American citizens. Rights tell us what we're entitled to, and laws tell us what we can get away with. But neither can make us treat each other in any particular way. They can set a baseline of what Americans can and cannot do, but they cannot legislate love. As Pastor Andy Stanley points out, just as traffic laws can't make us courteous drivers, and our right to free speech can't make us speak respectfully, neither can they make us love one another the way God has called us to.[10] Only a transformed heart can do what our rights and laws cannot.

The apostle Paul affirmed both our freedoms and our rights when he said that "everything is permissible, but not everything is beneficial" (see 1 Corinthians 6:12). In other words, we should never use what God's given us to indulge our flesh, because doing so is rarely beneficial—in fact, it often wreaks havoc. As applied to politics, that means while we *can* get away with treating people any way we want, we shouldn't. Because even though less-than-loving treatment is permissible, it violates God's commandment to love, and is therefore harmful to us as well as those we treat poorly.

We can't legislate unity any more than we can legislate love. These are higher laws of God, not of humanity. As Americans, we have every right not to love those we disagree with. But as Christians, we've given up our right to be anything less than loving.

**Make it personal.** In his book *Love Your Enemies*, Arthur Brooks shares a story about a speech he delivered. At the time, Mr. Brooks was the president of the American Enterprise Institute, a conservative think tank in Washington, DC. While speaking to a like-minded group, he "made the point that liberals are widely considered to be compassionate and empathetic, and that conservatives should work to earn this reputation as well." After his speech ended, a woman walked up to him looking upset and told him that he was being too nice to liberals. "'They are not compassionate and empathetic,' she said. 'They are stupid and evil.'"[11]

Her words evoked a strong reaction in Mr. Brooks, who grew up in Seattle, was raised by liberal parents, and had many liberal friends. Her attacks felt personal to him because she had denigrated those he loved most.

The two lessons he gleaned from this story were: (1) when we personalize what we say or think about those on the other side of the aisle, we're a lot kinder to those we disagree with politically; and (2) when we love people, we stand up for them. Every one of us has friends and family who hold different political beliefs than we do—people we love deeply, no matter how significant our disagreements may be. Denigrating the groups they're affiliated with denigrates them as well. Therefore, we should not sit idly by while people disparage others. Instead, we should remind them that they, too, have friends and family members who fall into the category of those they're disparaging.

Sometimes, however, a gentle rebuke won't get our point across. That's when we confront divisive people as directly and lovingly as we can. As Scripture says, we are to "take no part in the unfruitful works of darkness, but instead expose them" (Ephesians 5:11 ESV). The first step is confronting them personally to clarify and bring what they've said to light. If that doesn't stop them, Scripture gives us clear directions on how we should treat them moving forward: "As for a person who stirs up division, after warning him once and then twice, have nothing more to do with him, knowing that such a person is warped and sinful; he is self-condemned" (Titus 3:10–11 ESV). Paul reiterates this sentiment in the book of Romans, saying, "Watch out for those who cause divisions . . . avoid them" (Romans 16:17 ESV).

**Don't give up.** There will come a time when we're tempted to quit, believing that our efforts to foster unity are just too difficult, time-consuming, or futile. Such thinking, however, denies God's power to transform families, communities, cities, and nations through a single person's commitment to loving well. It also underestimates the danger that division poses to us.

Richard Haass, president of the Council on Foreign Relations, addresses this danger in his latest book, *The Bill of Obligations*. When asked what keeps him up at night, interviewers expect him to reply with any of the following threats: China, Iran, North Korea, terrorism, cyberattacks, or another pandemic. His answer always surprises them: "The most urgent and significant threat to American security and stability stems not from abroad, but from within." This threat comes from "political divisions that . . . have raised questions about the future of American democracy and even the United States itself . . . mak[ing] it near[ly] impossible for the United States to address many of its economic, social, and political problems or to realize its potential."[12] A sobering observation, if ever there was one, from someone who's seen it all.

Galatians 5:15 affirms Mr. Haass's statements, declaring, "If you bite and devour each other, watch out or you will be destroyed by each other." We cannot continue on this path of division without destroying our nation and ourselves in the process. The mission is vital, the cause is worthy, and never have God-fearing Christians been more desperately needed in politics than now. The fate of our nation, and this world, depends on us.

## REFLECTION

1. How serious is America's political division to you?
2. What responsibilities can you assume to help unify our nation?
3. What's one thing you can do this week—or even today—to bridge division in your own sphere of influence?

## PRAYER

*Lord, I need your help to become a unifying force in politics. Help me see those I disagree with the way that you do. Strengthen me so that I will not quit in my wholehearted pursuit of unity. Use me however you want to bring your will for America into fruition. I'm all yours, and I'm ready to go—so please, Lord, send me. In Jesus' name, Amen.*

# ACKNOWLEDGMENTS

All glory and praise to my heavenly Father, His Son, and the Holy Spirit, without whom I am nothing (John 15:5).

My parents, Calvin and Grace Gitsham—You've supported, encouraged, and believed in me since the moment I was born. I owe everything I am and will ever become to both of you.

Mrs. Barbara VanPutten, Mr. Mike Keisling, and Mr. Doug Hambright—three formative mentors and teachers who helped shape my mind and soul. Thank you for showing me the love of Christ, even before I recognized it as such.

Professor Christian Potholm and Alex Ray—The New England catalysts who transformed me into the politico I am today. Thank you for encouraging me to "Just Do It!"

Karl Rove—Thank you for taking a chance on me as a fresh-faced twenty-two-year-old and for giving me a forever home in the Bush-Cheney family.

Warren W. Tichenor—Thanks for leaving me money under the keyboard and for opening doors that no one else would or could.

Attorney General John Ashcroft—Your faithful example of public service made a deeper impression on me than you will ever know. Thank you for always standing on the side of godly truth and righteousness.

Pastor Miles McPherson—Your desire for unity in the body of Christ is my greatest inspiration! You are a beast in the best sense of the word, and I value your friendship enormously.

Senator Tim Scott—Thanks for being a true friend in a town where friends are very hard to come by.

Jason Cabel Roe—You're the reason I ran, and I never could or would have done it without you.

P.C. Koch—Your loyalty and friendship have paved the way for me time and again in Washington.

Andy McGuire and Rachel McMillan—Thanks for believing in, teaching, and encouraging me, every step of the way.

# NOTES

**Foreword**

1. "Pastors Share Top Reasons They've Considered Quitting Ministry in the Past Year," Barna, April 27, 2022, www.barna.com/research/pastors-quitting-ministry.

**Chapter 1 Indivisible**

1. George Washington, "Washington's Farewell Address to the People of the United States," United States Senate Historical Office, September 19, 1796, www.senate.gov/artandhistory/history/resources/pdf/Washingtons_Farewell_Address.pdf.

2. James Madison, "Federalist Papers No. 10," 1787, www.billofrightsinstitute.org/primary-sources/federalist-no-10.

3. Alexander Hamilton, "The Defence No. 1," 1792–1795, www.founders.archives.gov/documents/Hamilton/01-13-02-0217.

4. John Adams, "Letter from John Adams to Jonathan Jackson," October 2, 1780, www.founders.archives.gov/documents/Adams/06-10-02-0113.

5. Michael Dimock and Richard Wike, "America Is Exceptional in the Nature of Its Political Divide," Pew Research Center, November 13, 2020, www.pewresearch.org/fact-tank/2020/11/13/america-is-exceptional-in-the-nature-of-its-political-divide.

6. Cameron Brick and Sander van der Linden, "How Identity, Not Issues, Explains the Partisan Divide," *Scientific American*, June 19, 2018, www.scientificamerican.com/article/how-identity-not-issues-explains-the-partisan-divide.

7. Dimock and Wike, "America Is Exceptional."

8. Dante Chinni and Sally Bronston, "Americans Are Divided over Everything Except Division," NBC News, October 21, 2018, www.nbcnews.com/politics/first-read/americans-are-divided-over-everything-except-division-n922511.

9. Dr. George Barna, "A National Moment of Truth: Whose Vision and Values Will Prevail?" Cultural Research Center at Arizona Christian University,

September 27, 2022, www.arizonachristian.edu/wp-content/uploads/2022/09/CRC_Americas-Values-Study_02.pdf.

10. James Goll, "Exposing the Religious and Political Spirit," God Encounters Ministries with James W. Goll, November 9, 2017, www.godencounters.com/exposing-the-religious-and-political-spirit.

11. Kris Vallotton, Facebook post, October 2, 2019, www.facebook.com/kvministries/posts/the-political-spirit-and-the-religious-spirit-have-at-least-12-things-in-common-/10156794273808741.

12. Benjamin Franklin, "From Benjamin Franklin to John Adams," October 12[–16], 1781, www.founders.archives.gov/documents/Franklin/01-35-02-0441.

## Chapter 2  Identity Politics

1. "Identity Politics," Stanford Encyclopedia of Philosophy, https://plato.stanford.edu/entries/identity-politics.

2. "tribalism," Cambridge dictionary, accessed March 5, 2023, https://dictionary.cambridge.org/us/dictionary/english/tribalism.

3. Daniel R. Stalder, "Tribalism in Politics," *Psychology Today*, June 18, 2018, www.psychologytoday.com/us/blog/bias-fundamentals/201806/tribalism-in-politics.

4. Stalder, "Tribalism in Politics," www.psychologytoday.com/us/blog/bias-fundamentals/201806/tribalism-in-politics.

5. Michael Grunwald, "The Party of No: New Details on the GOP Plot to Obstruct Obama," *Time*, August 23, 2012, www.swampland.time.com/2012/08/23/the-party-of-no-new-details-on-the-gop-plot-to-obstruct-obama.

6. Thomas Koenig, "Tribalism is Anti-American," *National Review*, July 24, 2021, www.nationalreview.com/2021/07/tribalism-is-anti-american.

## Chapter 3  Ambassadors of Heaven

1. "Naturalization Oath of Allegiance to the United States of America," U.S. Citizenship and Immigration Services, July 5, 2020, www.uscis.gov/citizenship/learn-about-citizenship/the-naturalization-interview-and-test/naturalization-oath-of-allegiance-to-the-united-states-of-america.

2. 5 U.S. Code § 3331

3. Dietrich Bonhoeffer, *The Cost of Discipleship*, 1st reprinted ed. (New York: Touchstone, 1995), 89.

## Chapter 4  Undistracted

1. Steven Stosny, "Why Purpose Is a Requirement for Happiness," *Psychology Today*, June 20, 2022, www.psychologytoday.com/us/blog/anger-in-the-age-entitlement/202206/why-purpose-is-requirement-happiness.

2. Rick Warren, *The Purpose Driven Life*, expanded ed. (Grand Rapids, MI: Zondervan, 2012), 21.

3. Warren, *The Purpose Driven Life,* 34.

4. Asad Meah, *34 Inspiring Jack Canfield Quotes*, www.awakenthegreatnesswithin.com/34-inspiring-jack-canfield-quotes.

5. Andy Stanley, "Why Can't We Be Friends," Sermon Central, August 23, 2011, www.sermoncentral.com/sermons/2-why-can-t-we-be-friends-andy-stanley -sermon-on-conscience-159740.

6. Andy Stanley, "Why Can't We Be Friends."

## Chapter 5 Unoffended

1. Lin-Manuel Miranda, Leslie Odom, Jr., "Ten Duel Commandments," Track 15 on *Hamilton: An American Musical (Original Broadway Cast Recording)*, Atlantic, 2015.

2. History.com editors, "Aaron Burr Slays Alexander Hamilton in Duel," History, accessed May 18, 2022, www.history.com/this-day-in-history/burr-slays -hamilton-in-duel.

3. Ron Chernow, *Alexander Hamilton* (New York: Penguin, 2004), 722.

4. Noah Rothman, "The Outrage Economy," *Commentary*, July 17, 2019, www.commentary.org/noah-rothman/the-outrage-economy-illusion.

5. Shannon Pettypiece, "Marjorie Taylor Greene Calls for a 'National Divorce' between Liberal and Conservative States," NBC News, February 20, 2023, www .nbcnews.com/politics/congress/marjorie-taylor-greene-calls-national-divorce -liberal-conservative-sta-rcna71464.

6. Julia Shapero, "Majorities of Both Parties Reject Greene's 'National Divorce': Poll," *The Hill*, March 8, 2023, www.thehill.com/homenews/house/389 0660-majorities-of-both-parties-reject-greenes-national-divorce-poll.

7. Carol Tavris and Elliot Aronson, *Mistakes Were Made (But Not by Me)*, 3rd ed. (New York: Houghton Mifflin Harcourt, 2020), 36.

8. Tavris and Aronson, *Mistakes Were Made*, 37.

9. Mfonobong Nsehe, "19 Inspirational Quotes from Nelson Mandela," *Forbes*, December 6, 2013, www.forbes.com/sites/mfonobongnsehe/2013/12/06/20 -inspirational-quotes-from-nelson-mandela.

## Chapter 6 Inoffensive

1. Chris Hutcheson and Brett McKay, "Man Knowledge: An Affair of Honor— The Duel," *Art of Manliness*, June 16, 2021, https://www.artofmanliness.com /character/knowledge-of-men/man-knowledge-an-affair-of-honor-the-duel.

2. "Woe." *Merriam-Webster.com Dictionary*, Merriam-Webster, accessed March 24, 2023, www.merriam-webster.com/dictionary/woe.

## Chapter 7 Unshakable

1. Brad Schmidt and Jeffrey Winters, "Anxiety after 9/11," *Psychology Today*, January 1, 2002, www.psychologytoday.com/us/articles/200201/anxiety-after-911.

2. Pew Research Center, "Two Decades Later, the Enduring Legacy of 9/11," September 2, 2021, www.pewresearch.org/politics/2021/09/02/two-decades-later -the-enduring-legacy-of-9-11.

3. Pew Research Center, "Two Decades Later."

4. Pew Research Center, "Two Decades Later."

5. John Adams, "Thoughts on Government," April 1776, https://press-pubs .uchicago.edu/founders/documents/v1ch4s5.html.

6. Alex Castellanos in Gordon Liao, "The Role of Fear in Politics," *Politico*, November 11, 2008, www.politico.com/story/2008/11/the-role-of-fear-in-politics -015502.

7. Alex Castellanos in Gordon Liao, "The Role of Fear in Politics."

8. Study Finds, "Fear Is Contagious—and People Actually Feel It More in a Crowd," *Study Finds,* February 1, 2022, www.studyfinds.org/fear-is-contagious.

9. Daniel Kahneman and Amos Tversky, "Prospect Theory: An Analysis of Decision under Risk," *Econometrica.* 47, no. 4 (March 1979): 263–291.

10. Khristi L. Adams, "Fear: The Root of Hatred and Great Enemy of Community," HuffPost, March 15, 2016, www.huffpost.com/entry/fear-the-root-of -hatred-g_b_9447196.

## Chapter 8  Tasty and Bright

1. Martin Luther King, Jr., *Strength to Love* (New York: Harper & Row, 1963), 37.

2. Amina Chaudary, "Interview: Desmond Tutu," *The Islamic Monthly,* June 17, 2012, www.theislamicmonthly.com/interview-desmond-tutu.

## Chapter 9  Wise as Serpents

1. Bob Whipple, "Trust but Verify," *Leadergrow*, www.leadergrow.com/articles /trust-but-verify.

2. Aimee Groth, "You're The Average of The Five People You Spend The Most Time With," *Insider*, July 24, 2012, www.businessinsider.com/jim-rohn-youre-the -average-of-the-five-people-you-spend-the-most-time-with-2012-7.

## Chapter 10  Judge Properly

1. Damian Costello, "Bob Marley's Journey to Justice, Joy, and (Ultimately) to Christian Faith," *America: The Jesuit Review*, May 7, 2021, www.americamag azine.org/arts-culture/2021/05/07/bob-marley-music-global-injustice-christian -faith-240617.

2. Bob Marley, "Judge Not," Produced by Leslie Kong, Beverly's Records, 1962.

3. Simon Makin, "We Accurately Weigh Up a Person's Character in 0.1 Seconds," *New Scientist*, September 28, 2016, https://www.newscientist.com/article /mg23130930-500-we-accurately-weigh-up-a-persons-character-in-01-seconds.

4. Emily Cogsdill, et al., "Inferring Character from Faces: A Developmental Study," *Sage Journals*, Volume 25, Issue 5, February 25, 2014, https://journals .sagepub.com/doi/10.1177/0956797614523297.

5. "Why Are We So Quick to Judge Others? Here's What the Psychology Says," *TRTWorld*, December 29, 2021, www.trtworld.com/magazine/why-are-we -so-quick-to-judge-others-here-s-what-the-psychology-says-53122.

6. Don Stewart, "Who Were the Herodians?" *Blue Letter Bible*, www.blueletter bible.org/faq/don_stewart/don_stewart_1318.cfm.

7. Alexander Pope, *The Poems of Alexander Pope*, ed. John Butt (New Haven: Yale University Press, 1963), 160.

## Chapter 11  Love Your Enemies

1. Lois Tverberg, "'Love Your Enemy?' Jesus' Most Radical Words Explained," *Our Rabbi Jesus*, February 25, 2022, www.ourrabbijesus.com/articles/love-your -enemy-jesus-most-radical-words-explained.

## Chapter 12  Speaking Truth in Love

1. The Four-Way Test, Wikipedia, https://en.wikipedia.org/wiki/The_Four -Way_Test.

2. Justin Nortey, "Most White Americans Who Regularly Attend Worship Services Voted for Trump in 2020," Pew Research, August 30, 2021, www.pew research.org/fact-tank/2021/08/30/most-white-americans-who-regularly-attend -worship-services-voted-for-trump-in-2020.

3. William Barclay, *New Daily Study Bible: The Gospel of Matthew 1* (Edinburgh, UK: Saint Andrew Press, 2001).

4. "Declaration of Independence: A Transcription," National Archives, www .archives.gov/founding-docs/declaration-transcript.

## Chapter 13  Dive In

1. Alexis de Toqueville, "Individualism in Democracy in America by Alexis de Toqueville," *Bartleby Research*, www.bartleby.com/essay/Individualism-In -Democracy-In-America-By-Alexis-PZS35WYWPR.

2. Quinnipiac University Poll, "Americans Have No Appetite for Politics at Thanksgiving Table, Quinnipiac University National Poll Finds," November 22, 2021, https://poll.qu.edu/poll-release?releaseid=3829.

3. Alejandra O'Connell-Domenech, "How to Talk about Politics with Family This Thanksgiving," November 23, 2022, www.thehill.com/changing-america /well-being/mental-health/3748301-how-to-talk-about-politics-with-family-this -thanksgiving.

4. Ray Nothstine, "Government and God's People," *Acton Institute*, July 5, 2011, www.acton.org/pub/religion-liberty/volume-21-number-2/government-gods -people.

5. Nothstine, "Government and God's People."

6. "Introduction to Daniel," *Institute for Creation Research*, www.icr.org /books/defenders/4866.

7. Annenberg Public Policy Center, "Americans' Civics Knowledge Drops on First Amendment and Branches of Government," September 13, 2022, www .annenbergpublicpolicycenter.org/americans-civics-knowledge-drops-on-first -amendment-and-branches-of-government.

8. Joshua Infantado, "12 Reasons Christians Should Not Be Involved in Politics." *Becoming Christians*, https://becomingchristians.com/reasons-christians -should-not-be-involved-in-politics.

## Chapter 14 The Third Option

1. Joseph Serwach, "Love and Truth: You Can't Have One Without the Other," March 27, 2021, *Catholic Way Home*, www.medium.com/catholic-way-home/love -and-truth-you-cant-have-one-without-the-other-52187ec47573.

2. "Declaration of Independence: A Transcription," National Archives, July 4, 1776, www.archives.gov/founding-docs/declaration-transcript.

3. Dictionary.com, Definition of "inalienable," www.dictionary.com/browse /unalienable.

4. Miles McPherson, *The Third Option: Hope for a Racially Divided Nation* (New York: Howard Books, 2018), 140.

5. Ellie Lisitsa, "The Four Horsemen: Criticism, Contempt, Defensiveness, and Stonewalling," The Gottman Institute, www.gottman.com/blog/the-four-horse men-recognizing-criticism-contempt-defensiveness-and-stonewalling.

6. Jennifer Delgado, "Psychological Blind Spots: What You Do Not Know about You Weakens You," Psychology Spot, www.psychology-spot.com/psycho logical-blind-spots.

## Chapter 15 United We Stand

1. Cathy Lynn Grossman, "Sunday Is Still the Most Segregated Day of the Week," *America: The Jesuit Review*, January 16, 2015, www.americamagazine .org/content/all-things/sunday-still-most-segregated-day-week.

2. Michael Lipka, "U.S. Religious Groups and Their Political Leanings," Pew Research Center, February 23, 2016, www.pewresearch.org/fact-tank/2016/02/23 /u-s-religious-groups-and-their-political-leanings.

3. Dr. Martin Luther King, Jr., *A Gift of Love: Sermons from* Strength to Love *and Other Preachings,* (Boston: Beacon Press, 2012), 50.

4. Billy Graham, *The Journey: How to Live by Faith in an Uncertain World* (Nashville: W Publishing Group, 2006), 212.

5. Elizabeth Knowles, ed., *Oxford Dictionary of Modern Quotations, Third Edition* (Oxford, UK: Oxford University Press, 2007), 213.

6. Andy Stanley, "Like Stars in the Sky," YouTube, July 1, 2022, www.youtube .com/watch?v=M3LCC119qY0.

7. Eric Geiger and Kevin Peck, *Designed to Lead* (Nashville: B&H Publishing, 2016), 2.

8. Robert E. Quinn, *Change the World* (San Francisco: Jossey-Bass, 2000), 183.

9. Geiger and Peck, *Designed to Lead*, 59.

10. Andy Stanley, "Like Stars in the Sky."

11. Arthur C. Brooks, *Love Your Enemies: How Decent People Can Save America from the Culture of Contempt* (New York: Broadside, 2019), 3.

12. Richard Haass, *The Bill of Obligations* (New York: Penguin, 2023), xi–xii.

**Denise Grace Gitsham** was born and raised at Travis Air Force Base in Northern California. Her mother is a Chinese immigrant who escaped communism in 1949, and her father is a Canadian immigrant who served twenty years in the US Air Force. As a member of a proud military family, Denise has a special appreciation for the liberties that enabled her parents to achieve the American dream. She also recognizes the personal significance of her favorite Bible verse: *To whom much is given, from him much will be required* (Luke 12:48 NKJV). This verse underlies Denise's lifelong commitment to public service.

Denise is a graduate of Bowdoin College and the Georgetown University Law Center. Prior to starting her own public affairs firm, she practiced law at K&L Gates and served as a presidential appointee at the White House and the US Department of Justice, as well as a law clerk in the US Senate. In 2016, Denise ran for Congress in California's Fifty-second Congressional District. Today, Denise advises businesses, ministries, and nonprofits as a consultant and board member.

Denise speaks Mandarin Chinese, is an avid reader, and has competed as an Ironman triathlete. When she isn't on a plane headed to or from DC, she's basking in the California sun with her golden retriever, Jack.